MW00583728

VIDEO SMART
Make smartphone videos like a pro

PELPINA TRIP

PELPINA Publishing
Pelpina.com

DEDICATION

To anyone who believed in me when I said smartphone video
is the future. To the folks who kept telling me smartphone
video was just a fad: you made me work harder. To my
husband Rik for always supporting me in my silly dreams
(who writes a BOOK on making VIDEOS?) and our
children: I could not be prouder of you.
This one is for you three.

CONTENTS

PREFACE

"You're not actually going to use that, right?" the director asked as he pointed to my iPhone. It was 2014, and we were shooting a video for an international brand. Nobody I knew was using smartphones to shoot business videos. But my brand new iPhone had just arrived in the mailbox that afternoon. So, I put it on a selfie stick and brought it with me to the shoot in Amsterdam.

"Well, we're also going to use that camera," I assured the man, as I pointed to the camera operator with a professional camera.

This was the first time I brought my smartphone to a professional video shoot. What's interesting is that most of the footage that was actually used in the final video were shots I took with my iPhone.

At that time, bigger was better. For high-quality, effective business videos, you needed a big budget, a big crew, and a big camera. But I had been experimenting with my smartphone for years. In 2012 I used not only my DSLR, but also my smartphone when I was shooting a segment for a national TV news show. It's hard to imagine now, but back then I never dared to tell the TV crew that I was doing that (even though, with the right lighting and composition, no one noticed anyway).

It's unbelievable how the technology and the perception of this has changed. Smartphones have become completely ingrained in society. We use our phones to take pictures, send emails, and keep up with business and our family. But not everyone has truly discovered the camera yet. My goal is to enable everyone who has a phone in their pocket to use it to make good videos. You've got it on you anyway!

My mission is to give you the tools, knowledge, and confidence to be able to make business videos yourself.

As an early adopter of smartphone video, I regularly receive requests to share my expertise. I've trained thousands of people to make effective videos, and it's exciting to see people understand the benefits of filming with their smartphone:

- You don't need a big budget to create professional videos.
- You always have your smartphone with you.

- You have everything in one device: camera, edit app, publisher.
- The smartphone is light and small, which makes it easier to capture unique and creative shots.
- People tend to be less intimidated in front of a smartphone, which can be helpful during interviews, for example.

This book captures many years of experience to help you make professional videos to reach your business goals. Good luck and HAVE FUN!

Pelpina

PREPARING YOUR VIDEOS
CHAPTER ONE

Watch this video by simply holding your smartphone camera towards the QR code

Do you want to make goal-oriented videos and save time making them? Spend less time on shooting and editing? Then you need a good plan.

After almost every videomaking workshop I give, participants will tell me: "You were right. I should have planned better. It would have saved me a lot of time." So, trust me: This is the most important chapter!

Before you grab your camera, take a step back. Take the time to plan out your videos and save a lot of time, energy, and frustration afterwards. Planning your videos doesn't have to be complicated.

For each video, you need two things:
1) A video plan
2) A shot list

The video plan is the content of your video. The shot list shows the visuals. And trust me, this doesn't have to be an extensive plan with a lot of details. I like to keep things simple, so let's start out with a basic video plan, and a short shot list.

VIDEO PLAN

We'll start with the content of your video: the video plan. You might already have some fun ideas for videos you want to make; now you just need to give shape to those ideas. That's exactly what the video plan is for. *(If you have no inspiration, don't worry: I've got you covered! Check the video format canvas later in this chapter.)*

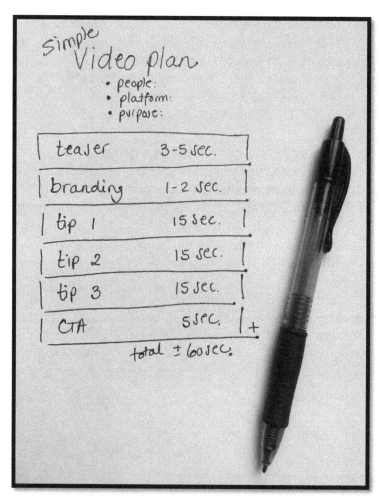

Simple video plan example

Each video plan has a few basic elements: the length of the video, the intro, the outro, how your video starts, whether it has subtitles, etc. First, I'm going explain the different basic elements, so that you can create your own (simple!) video plan.

Length of the video

One of the biggest factors that determines if your viewers are actually going to watch your video is its length! Do not underestimate this. Decide beforehand an approximate length of your video. At the end of this chapter, you can find specific info for the ideal video length per platform. But keep in mind that these specifications differ per target audience and change over time, so always keep up to date with the current guidelines and keep an eye on your own statistics.

The main questions you need to ask yourself: How long will my viewers watch my video? When and where (on wht platform) will my viewers likely watch this video? What is the right length for my ideal target audience?

Beginning of the video

Another big watch factor: the start of your video. What triggers your viewer to keep watching? What happens in the first few seconds? A few uninteresting ways to start a video: someone introducing themselves for more than 30 seconds (boring!), the exterior of a building (boring!), a full screen logo or a long paragraph of text (boring!). Some interesting ways to start a video: a powerful statement, an intriguing question, a unique product attribute shown visually, or a funny blooper.

Logo/branding

How is the logo or company branding visible in the video? This is another element you'll have to determine in your video plan. Most companies use a sound logo: a moving logo with sound or music that is visible for one or two seconds. (I know: I can hear the designers' and CEOs' doubts while I'm writing this sentence. Trust me: You really don't need the logo to be on screen longer than a few seconds.)

You can put your sound logo at the beginning of your video, but you can also put it after a fun teaser, or at the end of a video. You can also choose to have a small semi-transparent logo at the top or bottom corner of your video. Whatever you choose: make sure it matches your audience's expectations, and use the same branding style in every video.

"I always make a video plan. It helps me think about the creative shots I'd like to make, a possible start of the video, and a good ending. Every hour I spend in prep saves me at least two hours in editing."
Geertje Algera, Smartphone Video Expert

Video format

Landscape video is still the most common form of video.
It's well supported on almost all social media platforms,
and it's the standard format to film on almost every camera.
But vertical and square videos are on the rise, especially
when you want to reach viewers on LinkedIn, Instagram,
Tik Tok, or Facebook.

Vertical and square videos are a must for a young and
mobile audience. In the final chapter and in the overview
later in this chapter, you can find more on which format to
use for what platform.

Keep in mind that, again, these specifications differ per
target audience and change over time, so always keep an
eye on current guidelines and your own statistics.

Captions or no captions?

The answer to the question "Should I put captions in my
video?" is almost always YES.

Captions are a must. Most social videos are watched
without audio, and to accurately convey your message (and
to stop viewers from scrolling past your video), you need to
make it understandable without audio. Deaf and hard-of-
hearing people can only follow videos with good captions.
Plus, videos with captions are watched longer and receive
more interaction, so captions are good for SEO (Search
Engine Optimization). *How* you caption your videos is, of

course, a whole different topic. This is part of editing, which I tell you more about in chapter four.

Call to action (CTA)

If you filled out the video strategy canvas, you already thought about the general purpose of your videos. It is also really important to have a purpose for each individual video.

When the viewers watch this specific video, what are they going to do, think, or feel? Can you think of a short CTA? How does this call to action come onto the screen? Will it be supported by text and captions?

Visual and verbal call to action in a
LinkedIn video by Richard Moore

You might be tempted to close your video with a CTA, but as I said earlier, you don't have to save it for the end of the video. In fact, I'd recommend placing your CTA a bit earlier, since a lot of your viewers might be gone at the end of your video. Your video can also start with the CTA: "Hi, thank you for watching. Subscribe if you haven't!" You can also put it halfway through the video, "Before I continue with tip number three, did you know that I wrote a book on this topic? Check the link in the description below!"

So, take a moment to think about the right timing and placement of your call to action. What exactly do you expect of the viewer, and when would be a good time for your CTA to appear in your video?

Content of the video

What are you going to show in your video? Are you sharing your knowledge, is someone being interviewed, are you showing a product, or are you taking the viewers behind the scenes?

I always try to convey the message as clearly as possible. And I do this by breaking up the video in different parts.

If you want to save time during the video shoot, this is the part to pay careful attention to!

I hardly ever record even a two-minute video in one take. I always cut it into smaller pieces. This saves a ton of time on filming and editing.

Preparation is key. Let me give you a few examples of what not to do. Say you're making a video on a coworker who shares her knowledge on the operation of an airplane seat. Please do not write out a word-for-word script. I know it might be tempting to have control over the words, but a word-for-word script almost never comes across as natural. And in the end, if the message looks rehearsed, unnatural, or not real, it won't come across well, and your video will fail. So, the person in front of the camera conveying the message has to be able to do just that: convey the message. And that can be very difficult with a script that's written by someone else.

So, if you don't write the way you speak, what can you do? You can ask your coworker to share their knowledge while you simply record. But before you know it, your coworker talks for 30 minutes, and you're going to have to edit those 30 minutes into a 1.5-minute video. Ah, there's a new challenge! Now, editing the video will take you a long time. So that's not a very efficient way to work either.

Here's my advice: Cut your video up in smaller steps beforehand. For example, in three parts: the operation of the armrest, the folding table, and the screen. Since you know you'll want the final video to be about 1.5 minutes, you simply ask your coworker to talk about each part for

*Kim Swagemakers from KimPact creating a
video plan for her B2B Facebook group*

about 20 seconds. You'll then still have some time for the
intro/outro/sound logo. You can record every part
separately, so your coworker doesn't have to do the whole
video at once. This makes it easier for your coworker, and
the editor too: You simply put together the three ready-
made pieces!

The ending

Think of how the video will end. What will the viewer see or do when the video has finished? Should the viewer be pointed some-where else? Do you want to link to another video? Do you want your logo on the screen? Or will you end with a nice quote?

If you have a hard time thinking of a good ending, perhaps you can take a look at the way you're starting your video. How does your video start? Who is in the video? What can you see, and what question or statement do you hear? You can often end with this as well, which completes the circle!

On the next pages, you'll find a few examples of video plans. Feel free to use them as inspiration for your own video plans.

Notice how the plan breaks the video up in different smaller steps. You can use this in every type of video. Just keep in mind your ideal viewer (people), the place you'll publish it (platform) and your main goal (purpose).

So, don't just copy-paste the plans; every target audience and every video goal is different!

Event video

Example video plan

Start off with a good quote or a quick montage of event atmosphere shots

Intro event in text
with small logo 1.5 seconds

Montage of quotes and/or atmosphere shots

CTA clear throughout video (not just at end)

Name/company of the interviews should be featured clearly

End with logo and website landing page

Event video plan example

Product Video

Example video plan

Start off visually showing
a unique feature of this product

Title product
with company logo 2 sec

Introduce product

Show product, use graphics and text for
specific dimensions and attributions

Short summary of pros and cons

End with logo and product page website

Product video plan example

Business Vlog
Example video plan

Start off with a good quote,
funny blooper or catchy intro

Title vlog in text
with music

CTA: subscribe to our channel

Vlog shot in short separate shots

Ask a question to the viewers
halfway through the video

End: refer to other vlogs
logo & music

Business vlog plan example

Interview

Example video plan

Start off with a good quote or interesting moment of interview

Title interview in text with company logo 2 sec

Introduce topic, name/title of person in graphics

Interview questions

Ask a question by a viewer halfway through the video

End with logo and landing page website

Interview video plan example

VIDEO SHOT LIST

Apart from your basic video plan, you also need a basic shot list. Your video plan is your content; your shot list is the visuals.

How are you going to visualize your message? What are you going to show?

Now don't panic; making a shot list won't take a lot of time. For most of the videos I make, it literally takes a minute or two. But in the end, it can save a lot of time. Say you're at an event with a company booth, and you want to make a video impression. It can be difficult to focus on filming all the right shots while you're talking to people and exchanging business cards.

Before you know it, you're back at home, only to discover that you completely forgot to make a nice compilation shot, or you didn't take any shots of your booth. There's no way to redo them when the event is over.

To prevent this from happening, you simply need a list with the shots you want to take. So, when you're at the event, all you have to do is check your shot list – and you can then fully focus on talking to people and networking!

*Ellen van Dieren, recruitment expert, recording a B2B vlog
to be published on LinkedIn. Before she started, we created
a video plan and a shot list (which included showing her
planner). Her videos received over 100K views, hundreds
of comments, and resulted in several direct business leads*

On the next page, you'll find an example of a shot list for
an event video. Feel free to use this as inspiration for your
own shot list. But remember, don't just copy-paste; all
videos and target audiences are different.

Event Video
Example shot list

Wide, medium, close-up atmosphere shots of the building. Inside and out.

People talking, shaking hands, exchanging business cards.

Timelapse of event build up, people walking in room, event floor, etc

Shots to accompany the video's call to action (brochure, report, website, etc)

Branded shots: company booth, company products, employees at work,etc

Video shot list example

EFFECTIVE VIDEO TOPICS AND FORMATS

Perhaps you're not sure where to start. You might have no idea what kind of topics will work for your videos, or perhaps you have too many ideas.

Let's get focused!

Video vision

One of the first questions I ask every company/organization I work with is: Do you have a video vision?

It's great that you want to make videos, but what is your goal? How does video fit in your overall marketing strategy? What is the exact role of video in your company, what do you want to say with your videos, and what do you want to emit?

 If you want your videos to do something, you need to have a clear video vision with a specific goal in mind.

Each company or brand has a story, a core objective, or vision that all the company's activities are based on. Your company or brand undoubtedly has a goal: to sell the best kitchens in your state, to reforest the tropical rainforests, or to give all puppies in the shelter a new home.

Apart from the main goal, you also have secondary goals like generating views, becoming more visible, or raising money. All of these secondary goals contribute to reaching your main goal.

I can hear you think: sure, Pelpina, but where is this going? Well, if you don't have a specific goal for your video, you have no true control over the results. You need to have a clear video vision with a specific goal in mind. Videos are a great tool to tell your story and to show your vision to your client or target audience. But there's no point in spending time and money creating nice videos if you don't know what you want to achieve with them, or what your ultimate goal is.

Do you want to create brand awareness because people don't recognize or know your brand?
Or do you maybe want viewers to not immediately click away from your website, but stay a little longer? Or do you simply want to convert those video views into sales?

Really think about your video's specific, measurable business goal: number of views, downloads, awareness, shares, links, sales, etc. If you don't know what your goal is, you'll never know if your investment has been worth it.

To help you with your video vision, I've developed a video strategy canvas. You can find it on the next page, and you can also download it for free from my website: pelpina.com.

Filling out the canvas will take you a few minutes. It will give you an overview of your goals, and it can provide new insights to your video strategy.

The canvas in includes the 3P's, People, Platform and Purpose. In the next pages I will dive deeper into how to use this method to your advantage.

VIDEO FORMAT CANVAS

PELPINA
Video Smart.

People

Who is your ideal viewer?
Be specific.
What are questions, problems, themes of interest to your viewer?

What type of video would be of interest to your viewer? Who would they like to see? What problem should be solved? What information do they want?

Platform

Where does your viewer consume content? YouTube, Facebook, LinkedIn, Instagram, newsletter, website, platform?

What type of video works best for the platform you picked? Think about: length of video, start of video, use of subtitles?

Purpose

What do you want the viewer to: do, think OR feel while watching your video?

If you have a call-to-action, where and when does it appear in the video?

My goal with the video format canvas is to make you think about 3 Ps: People, Platform, and Purpose.

1. People

Always try to start with your people: your ideal viewers. Let's say your main goal is to sell kitchens. Don't just get your camera out, thinking "I want to sell more kitchens." Let's first think about your ideal viewers. Who do you want to reach with your videos? Who would buy your kitchens?

What is going on in the world of your ideal viewers? What are known questions, problems, themes?

What topics can your viewers relate to? Do customers have recurring questions that you could use for an FAQ video? Or are there certain themes/events that are coming up soon that you could make a video (or video series) on? Try to dive into the world of your ideal viewers to come up with good topics.

2. Platform

If you know who your ideal viewers are, you probably also know where you can reach them. Where do your viewers communicate? Where do they "live" online? Is it best to reach them on LinkedIn, YouTube, Instagram, or Facebook? Perhaps with a newsletter? Or WhatsApp?

Now that you know the first two Ps (people and platform), you can start shaping the format for your video; for example, how long your video is going to be, if you need subtitles, and if you're going to go for a horizontal, vertical, or square video.

For example, people generally tend to watch a lot shorter and more-focused videos on Instagram Stories, so short, to-the-point videos on current events would be suitable. LinkedIn is a good platform for knowledge videos, while longer, informative or entertaining videos work well on YouTube.
When I help companies or organizations with their video strategy, I always make a simple video overview.

On the next page, you'll find a simple social video overview I created for the communications department at Limburg, a Dutch Province. These are the guidelines we created after looking at their audience and statistics. Now, keep in mind that the guideline differ per audience and topic, and change over time. Please don't just copy-paste this overview to use for your own audience. Remember to always keep an eye on your own viewers, statistics, and current network's guidelines to make a fitting video overview.

Channel	Length	Square Version	Open Captions	Closed Captions	Thumbnail
Website	< 4 min.			X	X
YouTube	3-5 min.			X	X
Facebook	3 min.	X		X	X
LinkedIn	< 2 min.			X	
Instagram	Max 1 min.	X	X		
Twitter	Max 2.20 min.		X		
Intranet	2-3 min.			X	

Social video overview example

3. Purpose

What is the main goal of your video? What will your viewers do, now that they have seen (part of) it? Do you want your viewers to click on something, send in a picture, or go to a website? Then make sure to have that really come across. Think beforehand what your CTA, or "call to action," will look like, and where it is going to be in your video.

 What is the main goal of your video? What will your viewers do, now that they have seen (part of) it?

A CTA can be in the beginning, or somewhere in the middle of the video. You don't necessarily have to save it for the end. In fact, it's better if you don't: Most viewers will be gone by the end of the video. And keep in mind that a CTA doesn't always mean your viewers have to do something. Perhaps you want to make your viewers think differently, or feel something, or inspire them. These are all goals that don't necessarily require a call to action.

Now that you have covered the 3 Ps, you should have a good foundation for making efficient, goal-oriented business videos. Together with your video plan and shot list, you can now start making videos!

Ready? Let's go!

FILMING
CHAPTER TWO

Watch this video by simply holding your smartphone camera towards the QR code

AUDIO TIPS AND TECHNIQUES

Summer 2009. I was about to interview one of my idols, tech celebrity: Shira Lazar. She had her own TV show, and I had been following her for some time with great interest. After many emails, I managed to get an interview with her for my video podcast "WebBeat TV." I was thrilled to be talking to her. She didn't have much time, of course; the whole thing was supposed to only take 10 minutes.

After many preparatory talks, the moment was finally there. I was so grateful to be able to have her on my video podcast. And of course, I was also very, very nervous. This had to be done in one take, and we only had a little bit of time with her. So, one more light check. One more camera check. I had folded the piece of paper with questions about 52 times. I had already gone to the mirror three times to check my hair. We checked the focus one more time. Yes. We were ready.

The interview went well. In the beginning I was a little nervous, but because of Shira's professionalism, we quickly got going. About halfway through, I didn't even look at my notes anymore. It turned into a fun conversation with nice quotes and beautiful pieces for my video podcast. That's what I *thought*.

After the interview, my editor walked up to me with a red face. There were some audio issues: Shira Lazar's audio was going in and out throughout the conversation. Because of this, we weren't able to use big chunks of the interview. What were we going to do? We couldn't possibly voice-over Shira's part, and it was impossible to ask her for another interview.

In that moment, I wished the earth would swallow me up. What a horrible mistake. Eventually, after taking a long time to puzzle the usable parts together, we were able to make a usable video podcast out of it.

But still, it wasn't what it could have been. And right then and there I learned one of the biggest lessons in video-making: without good audio, you don't have an interview.

Because of my enthusiasm and nervousness, I forgot my basic checks, which are always: audio, light, camera.

 Before I hit record, I check these three things:
audio, light, camera.

For every video, whether it's with some kind of celebrity or a small vlog shot at home, I check these three things: audio, light, camera. They're simple, short checks. But if you forget them, or in your enthusiasm pass over one check, it can cost you a lot of time and frustration. My advice is to start every production with these basic checks. So, let's start with, you guessed it: audio!

*A simple audio check usually takes a few seconds
but can save you a lot of time in the edit*

Listen to your surroundings

What did I learn from the interview with Shira Lazar? You
can't redo audio. Audio needs to be right the first time. So,
before I take out my camera, I always do an audio check.
This can be as simple as listening to my surroundings.
When I'm shooting somewhere, I'm always very conscious
about the ambient sounds. What do I hear? Am I in a quiet
hospital where people are whispering, and we're able to do
an interview?

Am I in the middle of an outdoor event with music and people talking? Or am I in an industrial building that has a ton of echoes?

What do I hear around me? And can I change any sounds that might be distracting?

Perhaps I can to go to another area, shut the windows and doors, turn off the TV, or get rid of or lessen the noise of other sources.

What does the space look like where I want to shoot? Is there carpeting? Are there curtains? If the audio is bounced back onto flat surfaces like windows, floors, or tables, it can create reverb. If the audio gets "absorbed" by fabrics or soft surfaces like carpets and blankets, it results in a warmer sound. This is also the reason I have a couple of blankets in the trunk of my car. Not to camp at any moment (also fun), but to make the audio better during shoots. Simply put a few blankets on the floor/tables in the space you're recording, and you immediately hear a difference in audio!

Microphones

Unfortunately, you're not always able to change ambient sounds. Sometimes it's just not possible to move to a different location, shut windows/doors, or put down blankets. When you're at an event, you can't ask everyone to be quiet.

That's why I always advise people to use a microphone. When used well, a microphone can guarantee good audio, and you don't have to worry about the wind as much, or turn down the noise from the TV in the background. There are different kinds of microphones, and the best one to use depends on the situation and the kind of video you're producing.

Lavalier microphones

I usually use a lavalier clip-on microphone, because for most videos I make I'm in front of the camera by myself. I plug the microphone directly into my phone, and I don't have to worry about sounds of cars or children playing outside. A lavalier microphone is ideal for videos that don't require a lot of walking, or mainly have one person in the shot.

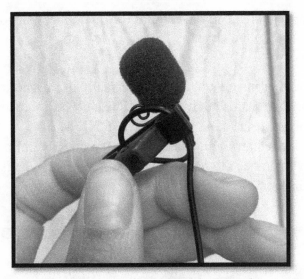

Lavalier microphone Rode Smartlav

There are a ton of different kinds of brands and types of lavalier microphones. When I used to shoot a lot on a DSLR camera, a Canon 60D, I used a wireless Sennheiser set. These days I mainly use the Røde Smartlav+ and Rode Wireless Go for my smartphone. (No, Rode does not sponsor me. I wish!)

Reporter microphones

In situations where it's all about spontaneous interviews, however, such as at an event, a lavalier microphone isn't always the best option, mainly because it can take some time to put it on.

Also, most lavalier mics are omnidirectional, which means they pick up sound from all directions. Reporter microphones are usually cardioid, which means they only pick up sound directly in front of the microphone, ignoring most background noises.

At events or in street interviews, I usually use a reporter microphone that is ready to use and can capture someone's natural enthusiasm. As I mentioned, this kind of microphone narrowly focuses on what's directly in front of it, so you do need to really point it at the person who is speaking.

Interviewing video expert Jeremy Vest at Vidcon 2019

Shotgun microphone

You can also use a shotgun mic that you simply attach to your phone and point at whatever or whomever you want to film. A shotgun microphone is useful when you make a lot of videos on the go, when you move around, or when you do spontaneous interviews with multiple people. Another benefit of the shotgun microphone is that you, or the person you're interviewing, aren't attached to your phone with a wire. Great for on-the-go!

Shotgun microphones are supercardioid, which means they are really good at picking up sounds from a specific point and ignoring other sounds. It also means it is really important the mic is always pointed towards the person being interviewed. Sound monitoring when using shot a shotgun microphone is therefore more important than when using an interview microphone.

Shotgun microphone

Earbuds as a backup

I bring a backup microphone for each shoot. And the backup of my backup are the white earbuds you get with your iPhone. Those earbuds actually have a decent microphone. One time, I led a smartphone video shoot at the Dutch Forensic Institute. The interview had been set up, the phone was ready to record on the tripod, but then we couldn't get the microphone to work. We eventually used the iPhone earbuds and taped them to the T-shirt of the guy we were interviewing (all the things duct tape can be used for). The end result? A nice closeup (the earbuds have a short cord) with good audio!

Tips for buying a microphone

When purchasing a microphone, pay attention to these things:
- Is the microphone compatible with your smartphone? Double-check the description and connector.
- What kind of microphone are you looking for: lavalier, handheld, or a shotgun mic? What kind of videos will you mainly be making (interviews, vlogs, or event reports), and what kind of microphone is useful for that?
- Do you want a wired or wireless microphone?
- Does the microphone come with a wind-screen?
- Can you use the microphone without having to download extra apps?

No external microphone

You don't have to buy a microphone, of course; you can also just use your phone's microphone. One of the best-known innovators and inspirers in the field of mobile journalism is Yusuf Omar, who doesn't use external microphones or tripods.

"Believe it or not, I don't use anything. I don't use a tripod, I don't use a microphone. I get close to people and put my phone right close to their lips."

Yusuf Omar, multi-award-winning mobile journalist and smartphone video expert

If you are not familiar with Yusuf's videos from "Hashtag Our Stories," definitely check them out. They're a great example that the quality of the story, your message, is what truly matters. I'm personally still not quite over my Shira Lazar blooper, so I do always carry a microphone!

 To see the products that I'm currently using, including microphones, download the free smartphone gear sheet on my website: pelpina.com.

Audio check

To ensure good audio, always do a quick audio check. It's not complicated and usually doesn't take longer than half a minute, but in the end it can save you a lot of frustration and time.

Simply go to the place where you want to record your video, and do a test for about 10 to 20 seconds. Have the person who's in front of the camera say a couple of lines, and then listen to the recording. Does the audio sound good?

It's simple, but it works. You really just need to make a habit of it. The more you do an audio check before you record, the faster this will be part of your routine when you're shooting a video.

Of course, also be alert to the surrounding sounds while you're shooting. When a truck passes by, or there's a sudden wind flare, be sure to listen to the recording right then. It's better to check one time too many than not enough. I can recommend using headphones for checking audio in noisy environments. You can even consider investing is professional sound monitoring headphones, if you film a lot in loud or noisy places.Remember the Shira interview: You can't redo audio later. It has to be right the first time!

Music

Music and/or a sound trademark are also part of audio. Music can greatly influence the style and tempo of your video, so it's really important to choose music that suits your goal and brand. And music is also something that you have to be careful with: You can't just put your favorite Alicia Keys song under your video due to copyright.

Music is part of your brand

Most of the companies I start working with do not have a music track or a sound trademark. While a lot of companies spend plenty of time and money on just the right logo and a perfect website – they usually don't spend a lot of time or money on music, or audio design. They manually search for music for every one of their videos. Which means all videos have a different music track, and therefore a different 'feel.'

Another way to do it, is look at music as being part of your brand. Music is such a big factor in determining the rhythm and feeling of your videos. Just like a logo, font, and website: music and/or audio design should be a part of your brand.

 Music is such a big factor in determining the rhythm and feeling of your video. Music is a part of your brand.

And making music a part of your brand doesn't have to be very difficult. My advice is to buy a couple of music tracks or have some made that you can always use in your videos. Check epidemicsound.com, Audiojungle.com or Pond5.com, or simply google for copyright -free music tracks. Once you've got a set playlist of music to choose from (this can be one track, but it can also be a library of songs), you ensure that the music fits within the brand of the company. Plus, you don't need to spend a lot of time searching for music each time you make a video.

A few tips for finding the right music:
- Music taste is personal. Find something yourself that fits the company and the brand.
- Music should not distract from the video's main message.
- Make a folder with a few music tracks for different video series/goals that different people on the team can access.

Go for quality

Because music is a part of your brand, my advice is to buy a good quality music track. Free music is usually not only of lesser quality, but spend 20 minutes on YouTube, and you hear the same kind of free music tracks in all videos.

When you buy a music track, you usually receive a package with different versions: a three-minute track, a one-minute track, a 30-second track, and just a "pling" or "swoosh." This definitely comes in handy for different kinds and lengths of videos.

Even better than buying existing tracks is having personalized music made. Look for a company that'll make a unique sound that completely fits your company and brand. You can have this done at agencies, or you can look for freelancers.

Jingle or brand sound

Of course, you don't necessarily need to have music in all your videos. Maybe a jingle or a short sound that represents your company is enough. A jingle is usually a moving logo with sound: a short bit of music. A brand sound can also be a "swoosh," "pling," or another sound that fits the branding of your company.

LIGHTING TIPS AND TECHNIQUES

Do you remember the basic checklist?
1. Audio
2. **Light**
3. Camera

We've covered audio, so now it's time for lighting, because with the right lighting, you can make your video look more professional in an instant. Just moving a few inches or simply turning around can make a massive difference.

This might sound easy, and it is, but so often I see videos where the angle of the lighting could've been slightly different, which would make the video look so much better.

 And just like with audio, light really needs to be right the first time.

Sure, you can edit it a bit afterwards, and throw on some filters, but trust me: If you have harsh shadows on your face, you simply can't delete the shadows in the edit. Lighting needs to be right the first time.

Outdoor lighting

The best light? That's right. Daylight.

I've never met anyone who looks pretty under fluorescent office lights. And yellow lights can give a nice, warm, romantic effect, but might not be a good fit for business videos. So, if possible, and if it's relevant to your videos – go outside! Did you find a good recording spot? Make sure to check the light. Where is the light coming from? Where is the sun in relation to your subject?

Light check

Always do a short light check. It will eventually become part of your routine and is pretty simple: It's usually a matter of walking and turning around.

- Where does the light come from? (Where's the sun?)
- How does the light fall on your face, or on the person you're interviewing? Can you see the eyes well? This is important: Eye contact is how we human beings make contact!
- How does the light fall on objects or on landscapes?
- Turn, move a couple of feet, hold the camera higher/lower: What does this do to the lighting?

Direct sun

Shooting in direct sunlight can be tricky. On a sunny, clear day, bright sunshine can create harsh shadows on objects or faces.

In case you're shooting during the day while the sun is shining brightly, it's best to look for indirect sunlight. Just look at the next two pictures, each taken at the same location, just a few meters apart.

Bright sunlight can cause harsh shadows and eyes to squint. Moving to indirect sunlight (sometimes just a few feet) can have an instant effect!

Golden hour

Have you heard of the golden hour? Every photographer or videographer is familiar with it. The golden hour is in the early morning or early night, when the sun rises or sets and everything around you gets a nice golden glow. Shadows become less harsh. It can create beautiful, soft lighting and nice warm colors.

With this in mind, you could plan your video shoot around the golden hour, especially if you're looking for nice fill shots of landscapes or nature.

The golden hour can create a nice golden glow, soft shadows, and warm colors

Lighting techniques indoors

When I receive a request for a video production that needs to be shot mainly inside, I visit the location, or I ask for pictures of the location before the video shoot takes place. This way, I know the lighting situation beforehand, and that's crucial: The right lighting will make your videos look a lot more professional.

In front of a window

If you're making a vlog or short video with your smartphone, make sure to correctly use the light sources around you. Simply moving a few feet can make your video look a lot more professional. The simplest solution: Stand in front of a window. Never stand with your back to a window or other light source, because you get the opposite effect: You become a dark silhouette.

These pictures were taken in the same spot, right after each other. The only difference is the way I faced the window!

In case it's impossible or impractical to shoot by a window, it's also possible to use lights. You'll want to use continuous lights, and there a few solutions for this.

Clip-on lights

There is a variety of lights that you can clip on your camera or phone, which are especially useful for on-the-go videos. When purchasing, it's good to check the Lumen amount, and the power and brightness of the clip-on light. I personally love my Manfroto light and the Lume

Cube (very bright, so you can also use it as a fill light). Nowadays, you can buy anything online, and I've definitely made some bad gear purchases. One of them was a clip-on light that was so weak it didn't improve the video at all.

Clip-on light also have a disadvantage as lighting comes from a single source, which can result in shadows. They can be great for fill in light to complement other light sources already available (such as a window), but when the surroundings are too dark, clip -n lights have their limitations.
So, check the power and brightness of the light before buying!

Freestanding LED lights

Do most of your videos take place in different locations? Then LED lights on a tripod might be a good solution for you. Personally, I have three LED lights that I simply throw in my car before driving off to a video shoot. They're small and don't weigh much, and most importantly: produce nice lighting. Most LED lights have a wire, so if you want to be extra flexible about where you shoot, buy battery-powered LED lights.

Softboxes

My favorite. I personally think that softboxes mimic natural lighting best; they create nice, even lighting. I have a couple of softboxes in my workroom. The biggest downside to these lights is that they take up more space, and that it's a bit of work to put them together/take them apart for every shoot. So, in my opinion, softboxes are mainly useful for a fixed shooting location or high quality productions.

Construction lights

Low-budget solution? Construction lights! Construction
lights produce nice white light. But, be careful; they can get
very hot. (Don't put anything too close to one. I
unfortunately still have burn marks in my staircase carpet.)
Construction lights also produce really bright light, so you
definitely can't look directly at the light during shooting.
My advice is to bounce the light off a white wall for
indirect lighting.

Three-point lighting

The best way to light someone is through three-point
lighting. It's a really simple technique used in photography,
videography, and movies. The principle is simple: Light a
subject with three sources from different angles.

- *Key light:* The main light (slanted) at the front
- *Back light*: From behind, to pull the object/person
  away from the background and remove shadows
- *Fill light:* To fill in any remaining shadows

This way, you prevent unwanted shadows and pull the
subject away from the background.

"I have attended events where I actually took an entire suitcase full of video gear. Because of my iPhone, I can now carry all my gear in a small camera bag. I love using my iPhone to shoot my video, and use it every day to do so."

Gary Leland, host and producer of "The four minute Crypto show" and the fastball softpitch TV show" using 3-point lighting

Now I can hear you think: Do I really have to always use three lights?
No. I absolutely understand you probably won't always shoot with three lights. I hardly ever do!

But, it is good to know how to light your subject properly, and if you keep getting unwanted shadows in your video, you now know why: It's probably because you need more light sources.

So if you want to build a temporary studio inside, and you can't seem to get the lighting right – or you keep seeing shadows behind the person – it might not be the lights, but more so the technique: Are you lighting the subject or person the right way?

Like I said, it's not necessary to always light your subject this way.

 Use daylight when possible, and if you're shooting inside and are using lights, use white lights!

Practical lighting tricks

Have you ever filmed someone and all you could see on the screen were bright white lines all over their face (completely overexposed)? Or the opposite: The background was nicely lit, but the subject was just a dark blot?

The best way to prevent these issues is by telling the camera which object the exposure should be set to.

Lighting settings

On most phones, exposure and focus is linked in together. So, if you focus on a flower – the light settings are automatically adjusted to that flower as well. Changing the exposure is generally done the same on most smartphones: Simply tap the main person/product on your screen.

If you're standing in front of the camera yourself, you simply tap your eyes. If you're filming a landscape, you can tap different spots (the tree in the foreground, the grass in the background, or maybe the sky). You'll see that the phone then adjusts and optimizes the exposure to your chosen object. Neat!
Usually, simply tapping your screen to adjust the focus/exposure works fine. But in some cases, you simply cannot get the desired results, because you cannot get the ideal focus and exposure combination. That's when you have to manually adjust the exposure.

Tap your screen to change the focus and exposure

Manually adjusting the exposure

You can also manually adjust the exposure (light settings) on your smartphone. On iPhones, after you tap the screen to adjust thee focus, simply move the yellow sun up or down. On most Android phones, you can move a lightbulb to adjust the lighting.

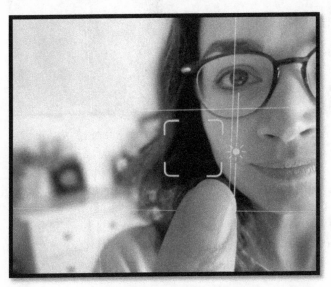

Move the sun (iPhone) or lightbulb (Android)
to adjust the lighting

Do you want to keep the exposure he same throughout the shoot? Keep your finger on the spot you want well lit (simply tap the screen) and hold for about two seconds. You'll get a notification that says something like "AE/AF lock."

Hold your finger in place for two seconds to lock the
exposure and focus (works on most phones)

The light/focus settings will now remain this way throughout the recording. If you want to unlock, simply tap
elsewhere on the screen. Do note that this is different
depending on your phone (it doesn't work on every phone
and in some phones, it only works on the rear camera).

If you want more control over the lighting, I can definitely recommend the app "Filmic Pro." This is a paid app, but it gives you a lot more control than most camera apps; Filmic Pro allows you to set the exposure and focus separately.

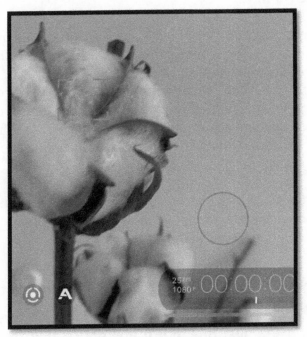

Focus (square) and exposure (circle) can be set separately in the app Filmic Pro

Colors & white balance

Something I had to do before every video podcast-shoot I did: hold up a white piece of paper. I had to hold it in front of the camera for a few seconds, so the camera operator could do what is called a "white balance."

Your smartphone is, of course, pretty smart and will do the white balance for you. For most videos, you absolutely don't have to worry about changing the colors. But if you find yourself filming with your phone and the colors look off, here's why.

All light sources have a color temperature (measured in Kelvin, thanks to the genius scientist who came up with this system). For every situation – daylight in the sun, inside at the office, or outside in the shade of a tree – color has a different temperature. Colors with a temperature close to direct sunlight appear as white, lower temperatures have a red/yellow hue, and high-color temperatures appear more blue/green.

So, colors look different in each situation, and the camera on your phone tries to capture the colors accurately according to the situation.

 Usually your phone captures colors just fine, but if you notice that the colors are more yellow or blue than in reality, you can adjust it.

By doing a white balance, you basically tell your camera what is white: what color is neutral. Based on that color white, the camera can decide what other colors should look like.

Usually, showing the camera something white (like a T-shirt or white piece of paper) does the job. The camera will often automatically adjust the colors. Most phones also have different light settings (sunny, cloudy, indoors) you can use. And if you want to be able to do a manual white balance, there are several white balance-apps, such as the app "Filmic Pro," which I mentioned before.

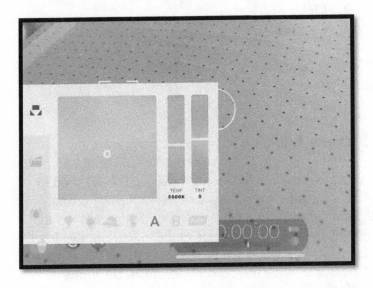

Change the color temperature and white balance with the app Filmic Pro

Like I said earlier, for most video shoots, you don't have to worry about white balance. But if you do think the color in your video is off, do a quick white balance. And think of me when you're standing in front of the camera holding up a piece of white paper!

CAMERA TECHNIQUES

Do you remember the basic checklist?
1. Audio
2. Light
3. **Camera**

We've done audio and light, so let's move on to camera techniques.

Camera framing

Vertical video was "not done" in 2012. When I used to train companies in making their own videos, I actually told them to never, ever shoot vertical videos because of the ugly black bars on both sides of the video. But that has all changed. Now, most people watch videos on their phone and vertical video has become accepted. On some platforms, it's even the ideal, must-use format.

 Whether to shoot horizontal, square, or vertical depends on the platform you will be posting your video.

To know what platform you should optimize for, you first need to know who your ideal viewer is. (Yes, we're going back to the three Ps from chapter one!) Who is your ideal viewer? Where do they spend a lot of time online? What is the right platform to reach them?

Horizontal videos

Landscape videos work well for most purposes. And if I'm honest, as a longtime/traditional video producer (dinosaur, ahem?), I prefer landscape video for optimal framing and composition.

Film horizontally when:
- Your target audience mainly watches videos on desktop/laptop.
- The videos will be posted on Vimeo, a newsletter, or your own Video Management System, or on another system that mainly supports landscape videos.
- You're still not really sure whether you should shoot horizontal, vertical, or square. It's possible to crop horizontal to square, but it's a bit difficult to do the other way around!

Vertical videos

You can't escape vertical videos as a social video maker. Vertical video is a must on social networks like Snapchat and Instagram (stories). And it actually makes sense. Most people who use their phone to check their social feeds hold their phones vertically. So isn't it a bit odd to rotate your phone horizontally to record a video?

Film vertically when:
- Your target audience mainly watches social videos on mobile devices.
- Your videos are mainly made for Snapchat, Instagram Stories, LinkedIn Stories, TikTok, Facebook stories, or other vertical-first platforms.

Square videos

Almost all social networks have fully adapted to square video, and the newest apps all support it. And that's not surprising; Square videos (1:1) get more interaction and views than landscape (16:9) videos, mainly because they take up 78% more of a phone screen than landscape videos. Plus, square video is always presented at the right size: It doesn't matter whether the viewer holds the phone vertical or horizontal.

Most smartphones can't film in a square format. So, if you're shooting a video, and the goal is to make it square, always remember that the video will end up being square: Parts will be cropped out. If you want to ensure everything will be in the square video, here's a tip. During filming, cover the screen with tape/paper until you have your 1:1 screen.

Change the canvas size with the app InShot

Another solution is to use apps like Filmic Pro and Clips to shoot square video. Or, shoot horizontally and crop your video square after filming, with apps like InShot or Quik. You can, of course, also make your video square in most editing software (Final Cut Pro, Adobe Premiere, Camtasia, Filmora).

Ways to hold your camera

What are some of the best ways to stabilize your smartphone? What should you look for in a tripod, or is it ok to simply hold your phone in your hand?

Handheld

Handheld filming can be great for some purposes. Vlogs, Instagram Stories, and behind-the-scenes videos can be perfect to film by hand. Of course, the image moves more, you always have one hand occupied, and you can't stand too far from the camera. But these elements can create an informal, personal, casual atmosphere you might be looking for.

Handheld interviewing on the go:
fast, simple, and spontaneous!

Stabilization

One of the best ways to make your videos look more professional in an instant is by stabilizing the image. You can do this by simply putting your camera on something, like a shelf on the wall, a table, or up against your laptop screen. But the fastest and easiest way to get a nice, stable shot is by using a tripod, which come in all shapes and sizes.

Selfie Stick

Personally, I always keep a selfie stick in my backpack, so wherever I am I can stabilize my video. I use a selfie stick with legs (Benro BK10), so it can also serve as a little table tripod. This means that when I'm shooting vlogs, I always have my hands free and I'm able to stand a bit farther away from the camera.

Using the Benro BK10: a selfie-stick and tripod in one

Tripod

A regular tripod gives you more flexibility in camera placement. My advice is to look for a tripod that's able to shoot at least at eye level, and has a leveler. And when you're filming with your smartphone, you of course also need a smartphone mount to use with the tripod.

Interviewing with tripod at the Dutch Forensic Institute

When purchasing a tripod:
- Pay attention to the specifications when purchasing: Is the tripod also suitable for your specific phone?
- What is the maximum height of the tripod? Can you film at eye level?
- Pay attention to the weight, especially if you are filming at many different locations.
- For easy switching between landscape and vertical shots, check the Joby and Manfroto tripods for smartphones.
- Budget-friendly tripod alternative: Lightstand. Tall, collapsible, and light. Disadvantages: You can't use different heights per leg, and there is no leveler.

"If I'm creating quick content, I like to use my iPhone. I carry a mini tripod, LED lights and Rode microphones to be able to film videos or live-stream on the go."

Goldie Chan, LinkedIn Expert & Video Content Creator

Stabilization apps

In case you're filming somewhere with your phone without a selfie stick or tripod, you can prevent "shaky" images with apps like Hyperlapse, Emulsio, or DeShake. These apps have a built-in stabilization function, which cuts the sides off your video to absorb the shocks, but does result in some loss of quality. In my personal opinion, you generally don't notice it, unless you're going for high-production value. So, if you want to ensure "smooth sailing" during your recordings without a tripod, I can recommend to film with an app like Hyperlapse, Emulsio, or DeShake.

Mobile & camera stabilizer

If you shoot a lot of videos on the go and want to stabilize like a pro, I recommend you shoot with a gimbal. The mobile stabilizers of DJI, for example, ensure your video is smooth and calm. Stabilizers are available for regular cameras and also for smartphones. The good thing about the DJI Mobile stabilizer is that through a simple switch, you're able to shoot in both horizontal and vertical mode. Super nice for your Instagram Stories or Snapchat videos!

How to make a dynamic video

How do you make a video that's visually interesting, appealing to watch?

Say dog, see dog

Show what you're talking about in your video. You're making a video, not an audio podcast, so visualize!

If you're talking about a dog, show a dog. If you're talking about a fire truck, show a fire truck. Whenever you're talking about a product, idea, or subject, show it! This way, your video will come to life with visuals. It sounds really simple, yet I still see a lot of company videos with mainly a "talking head," only a person talking. I personally think this is one of the best parts of making videos: visualization. How are you going to visualize what you're talking about?

 You're making a video, not an audio podcast, so visualize!

And if your idea isn't tangible, how will you visualize it? Are you able to symbolize it? Or are you able to add text or graphics?

A-roll & B-roll

Back in the day, when we used actual film, we worked with an A-roll and a B-roll. They were basically two film layers that you would literally place on top of each other. These days, fortunately, it's all a bit easier, but the basic principle and the terms still exist.

Your A-roll is your main image: the fundamental part of your video. For example, an interview, presentation, or vlog. In business videos, the A-roll is usually a person who is speaking.

Say you're making a video about a biking event, and you interview a participant. The A-roll would be the interview: quotes in which the cyclist talks about the event. This interview is the basis of your video; it is basically what carries the video.

If you only use A-roll, you only have a talking head; you only see the cyclist. But you usually also want to see images of what the person is talking about. And that's where the B-roll comes in: supplementary images.

How do you visualize your story? Before you hit record, you need to know exactly what images will accompany the A-roll. You need to have an idea of how you will visualize your story.

As I explained in chapter one, I always work with a shot list: a short list with all the things I want to shoot. I make the list beforehand, so when I'm on location I can shoot fast and with focus.

Tips for making a dynamic video

How would you film the space you're in right now? Whether you're reading this book on the train, in your living room, or in the doctor's waiting room, if you'd get your camera out right now, how would you visualize the space?

That's the exact first assignment I give people at the beginning of a video workshop: "Film the room we're in." Most course participants put the camera at eye level and shoot the space at a long distance. In a way it makes sense to shoot at eye level and from a bit of distance, because this is how we usually see the room. But if you want to really show your viewer the atmosphere, the camera needs to be in different, perhaps unexpected, distances, and angles. Don't be afraid to put your camera high, low, at an angle, close up, and far away. In fact, if you want to make a dynamic and visually interesting video, you *have to* use different distances and angles.

Three shots that can help you with visual storytelling and make your video more dynamic:

1. Establishing Shot

The "Where am I?" shot. With the establishing shot, you show the viewers where they are. It's usually a wide shot that quickly shows the location.

Establishing shot example: overview of an area

It can be a city skyline, the outside of a building, a land-scape, or a wide shot of a certain area. I'm going to be honest: The establishing shot is not always the most interesting shot, but it can be helpful to get your viewer to understand the story or get across a certain look/feel. To make your establishing shot a bit more interesting, try placing the camera at an unexpected angle or distance. Instead of filming a landscape or building at eye level, put your phone on the ground and look up at the building diagonally, for example.

 To make your establishing shot a bit more interesting, try placing the camera at an unexpected angle or distance.

The establishing shot is usually placed at the beginning of a video, which is understandable, but has also become a bit predictable. So, try to experiment with placing your establishing shot a bit later in the video!

2. Movement

Without movement in your shots, your video becomes a slideshow of pictures. To prevent this, you need to find movement/action and capture it. This doesn't mean that you need to move the camera; you can keep the camera still while capturing movement.

Try to capture movement in your shots

What do you see around you? Do you see leaves dancing in the wind, children's hands playing in the sand, bees buzzing on a flower? Or inside: people walking in a hall-way, hands shaking, fingers typing, or feet tapping?

Find a nice angle and distance to capture the movement. Don't capture everything at eye level, but try to experiment by placing the camera up high, on the ground, super close, or farther away.

3. Shots with depth

You know those beautiful shots in videos where the foreground is in focus and the background is blurry? Video cameras with the right lenses can capture depth really well. Depending on the type of lens, you can focus on an object and get the background blurred.

Put your phone very close to an object, and tap the object to make the background blurry

While the smartphone options are somewhat limited, it's still possible to create a blurry background.

How to create a blurry background with your phone:
- Place your camera an inch or two from an object and make sure there is a bit of room behind the object.
- Simply tap the object on your screen. The object should be in focus, while the background becomes blurry.

- If you want to switch focus, you tap the background. You can also do this during recording. Then, the background is in focus and the foreground blurry.
- Hold your finger on the screen for a few seconds, and you might also be able to lock the focus. The focus will be kept the same during the entire recording. This works on most phones.
- That's how you create a professional-looking shot with just your phone!

So, try it out! Find a nice object, make a super closeup and blur the background. That little statue on your desk for example. That beautiful flower in the garden. Or that funny mug from a colleague. Capturing details with super closeup shots helps convey the atmosphere. Making a beautiful video is all about finding the right things to capture!

Shot with depth: foreground (mug) is in focus, background is blurry

Be creative

If your goal is to make a dynamic, visually interesting video with compelling shots, you need to be creative in how you use the camera.

The great thing about your phone is that it's super light and small: You can easily put it in a fridge (open the door for a cool shot!), on a selfie stick up high for an unexpected eagle-eye angle, on the floor to jump over it, tied to your bike, etc. Here are a few ways to check if you have enough variation in shots:

- Vary shots from far away and close up.
- Mix between shots from above and below.
- Use shots with movement and still shots.
- Use a variation in color combinations.
- Make sure to incorporate audio (don't just film the bicycle bell, ring it!).

Don't just hold the camera at eye level and long distance. You'll get typical shots like this one:

Typical establishing shot filmed at eyelevel

Instead, move around. Put the camera high, low, closeup, look for movement and different angles!

Vary your shots: close up and far away, high and low, and capture movement.

If you're out of ideas, here is a way to get some inspiration. Say you're filming a saltshaker. Try to force yourself to become creative by filming at least five shots from different angles and different distances. For example, shot one could be a medium shot of the saltshaker at eye level.

Try to force yourself to become creative by filming at least five shots from different angles and different distances.

For the second shot, change the distance (close up?) and the angle (label from a corner?). For the third shot, change the distance and angle again, and so forth. Use the previous list to vary your shots. Create movement by using the saltshaker and filming it from different angles and distances. Or put the camera under a transparent glass cup (different angle) and shake salt onto the glass (movement).

Put the camera at the same level as the product

Put the camera below the product and use movement

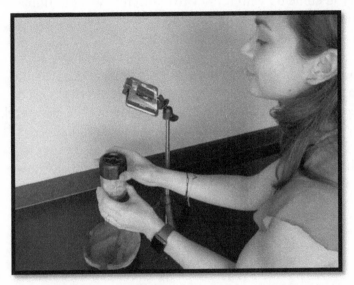

Put the camera above the product (eagle-eye) and use movement

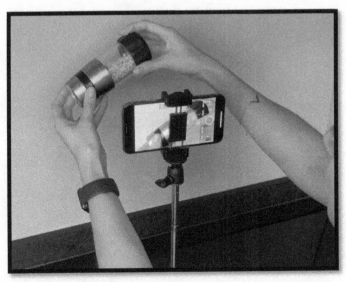

Use closeup movement

Try to come up with four or five different ways to film a product or person. With this simple trick, you basically "force" yourself to think outside the box.

You can apply this to almost any product or scene. Don't be afraid to move around the room, make super close-up shots, and think out of the box. Use different 'layers': work with something in the foreground and background.

That's when shots become more creative, and that's how you create a dynamic video!

IN FRONT OF THE CAMERA

CHAPTER THREE

Watch this video by simply holding your smartphone camera towards the QR code

Don't underestimate the power of the person in front of the camera. One of the biggest reasons your viewers will keep watching your videos: the people in it. Do I, as a viewer, believe what that person has to say? Do I like him/her? How does that person come across: self-confident, convincing, monotonous, or nervous?

That's why it's so important to capture people the right way. It's one of the biggest steps in ensuring your message comes across.

That's why, in this chapter, we dive into the art of filming people.

FILMING PEOPLE

Where do you place the camera? How close should you sit to the camera? And what about nerves – how do you come across naturally when you stand in front of the camera, but also how do you keep an interview casual?

Camera at eye level

I'm not very tall, so when I meet people for the first time, I always try to make myself a little taller, because we make contact with other people by looking into each other's eyes. Unfortunately, if someone is a lot taller than I am (which is often, considering I live in the Netherlands), standing on my toes doesn't really help my 5'3" self. That's why I love the camera: I can easily raise it to eye level and become as tall/short as the viewer in an instant!

Camera low: you look down on the viewer

If you place the camera low, you're looking down on the viewer. Even if the camera is just slightly lower than the eyes, the viewer will still subconsciously register it. This is a simple technique often used in film; place the camera low to make someone look powerful, big, or arrogant.

Camera high: viewer looks down on you

If you place the camera high, the viewer looks down on you, even if the camera is slightly higher than eye level.

This technique is used a lot to make a person seem smaller, powerless, or more childlike.

I know a lot of people take the most beautiful selfies from a high angle these days (goodbye double chin, and hellooo pretty light!). However, for business videos with a professional purpose, I recommend placing the camera at eye level. That's because when you meet someone in person, you also talk at eye level; it's the most natural way to have a conversation.

 Look at your canvas: this is your creative playing field!

Standard framing techniques

Look at your video canvas: this is your creative playing field! You decide where to put people in the frame – left, middle, right, close up, far away. Of course, there are standard framing and composition techniques, but let me say this first: Framing is subjective. What one person loves, another person might find awful.

Here are a few standard techniques.

Closeup

My personal favorite distance to shoot vlogs and interviews is close up. A standard closeup has a little space above the head with the shoulders visible. I shoot close up because my viewers mainly watch my videos on their smartphones.

The farther away I am from the camera, the smaller I'll be on the (already) small phone screen. People make a connection if they see your eyes!

Medium shot

If you want to show a little bit of the surroundings, a medium shot is perfect. A standard medium shot is from about the chest to right above the head. A medium shot and medium-long shots (see picture) can both be used for a reporter walking around at an event, because the viewer can see the environment as well as the reporter. The medium shot and the medium-long shots are also often used for interviews.

Long Shot

A long shot, also known as a "full body shot," shows the whole body from head to toe. It's a wide shot, usually used to show the environment. It's a perfect way to give viewers a feel of the location, but less suitable to make a personal connection with them. That's why I recommend using a combination of long shots and medium/closeup shots.

Common types of framing shots

Rule of thirds

Are you familiar with the video grid on your smartphone? The thin white lines in your camera screen divide the image into nine equal sections. It's also known as the rule of thirds, a widely used composition rule to help you decide where to place your subject in the frame.

This might sound complicated, but it's not. Research shows that a shot is more interesting when the subject is on one of these lines or intersections. So, to put it simply: You don't place the person in the middle of the frame, but rather a bit to the right or left side, on one of the lines. When you use the rule of thirds, you create space in your image, so the attention goes to the right part of the shot.

Use the rule of thirds while filming a person

Make sure you leave space at the correct side. That's why you have to check the viewing direction of the subject. If the person is looking to the left (so the person is on the right line of the grid), you keep an open space in the left part of the image.

On most smartphones, it's possible to turn the grid on while filming. On iPhones, go to your phone settings, camera, and then turn on the grid. On Android phones, go to your camera app, then settings, and then turn on the grid.

Background check

Once you have the person at eye level and you've decided on the right framing distance, you need to do a quick background check. You want the attention to be on the message, on the person. So, does the background add to the message, or does it distract? It's such a shame when you've shot everything and are ready to edit, only to find out that that there's a tree in the background "sticking out of the person's head." It's difficult to edit that out of the video!

You want the attention to be on the message, on the person. So, does the background add to the message, or does it distract?

Look into the lens

Do you know where the camera lens is on your phone? You might be able to point it out now, but when you film in selfie mode, do you look at the camera lens, or at yourself (on the screen)? It might sound silly, but most people who film in selfie mode look at themselves – not the camera lens. And that means they look past the camera lens. And that's a shame, because when you look past the camera lens, you look past the viewer. With vlogs, and usually with interviews, you want to look into the camera lens, because that's how you make direct eye contact with your viewer.

So why not turn the camera around? Well, shooting in selfie mode or with a flip screen can be very helpful, because you can see yourself, the background, and how long you've been shooting for. That's why I personally prefer to film in selfie mode when I'm filming by myself. But, as I mentioned earlier, it can also be distracting to constantly be confronted with your own face, especially if you're already a little insecure in front of the camera.

Post-it Note

If you're filming in selfie mode and feel completely distracted because you're constantly looking at yourself, here's a trick: Make sure you can't see your face anymore.

All you need is a Post-it Note, small cloth, or a piece of paper. And simply put it over the screen! Yes, it's as simple as that.

Wait to cover up your screen until after you make sure the lighting and framing are good, right before you start recording. This simple trick can help you to focus on the viewer, your story, and not yourself. My course participants often tell me this was one of the tricks that helped them the most. So, give it a try!

*Do you keep looking at yourself while filming? Put a Post-it
Note over your screen, so you can focus on the lens!*

INTERVIEWING

When you interview someone and you want the person to
look into the camera, make sure to tell them beforehand.
Don't just point to the camera, but also let them know who
they're talking to – the viewers. Then try to stand directly
behind the camera, so the person who is being interviewed
will look straight into the camera lens. If they still try to
make eye contact with you, take a few big steps to the left
or right, so that they can't look at you, and will look into
the camera lens.

Together in front of the camera

Are you sitting next to the person you're interviewing?
Or are you perhaps doing a quick vlog with two or three

people in front of a camera? Remember to look into the camera lens!

 Pretend the camera is another person joining the conversation, but not just any person – the *most important* person at the table.

If you're having a conversation, it's much more natural to look at the person(s) you're talking to. But if you don't look into the camera lens, you're not involving the viewer in your conversation. So, make sure to always start and end the video looking at the camera, and try to involve the camera (the viewer!) in your conversation.

Pretend the camera is another person joining the conversation, but not just another person – the most important person at the table. You do this by nodding, smiling, and talking to the camera lens. It might feel a bit unnatural to do at first, but keep practicing. Remember that you want the viewers to feel like you are talking to them; you want them to be a part of the conversation.

Interview framing

Think about the composition of interview shots before you go out on the interview: how far the camera will be from the person, if he/she is going to look into the camera or past the camera to the interviewer. Here are some of the most-used interview composition shots.

Looking past the camera

The person you're interviewing is looking past the camera to the interviewer. This usually results in a pretty natural conversation because the person who is being interviewed can talk to another human being, the interviewer. It's a great for people who are not used to talking to a camera. When you're filming by yourself, my advice is to use the front camera of your phone (selfie camera), so you keep an eye on the composition, lighting, and video duration while recording.

Being interviewed looking past the camera

Looking at the camera

The person you're interviewing is looking in the camera lens. This composition shot is perfect to connect with the viewer and make a video feel more personal, because of the direct eye contact.

At the same time, talking to a camera can feel like an unnatural way of communicating. So if the person who is being interviewed is nervous or not used to talking to a camera, this can be a bit tricky.

 Remember, you never talk to a camera. You talk to a person.

My advice is to help the person you're interviewing feel comfortable. Tell them they're not talking to a camera, but a person (and tell them who that person is). There are several different ways to do this, I'll talk about two.

The first way is fo you, as the interviewer, to stand directly behind the camera. If you stand next to the camera, the person you're inter-viewing will probably look at you every once in a while, which will be noticeable in the final video. So, try to become one with the camera, and stand at exactly eye level behind your phone. This way, the person can look directly into the camera and talk to you at the same time.

The second way is for the interviewer to stand several feet to the left or right of the camera. If the person in front of the camera still tries to make eye contact with you, and therefore keeps moving their eyes or looking past the camera, take a few big steps to the left or right. It's a simple way to "force" the person to look at the camera instead of at you.

Joseffa Trip (yes, my awesome sister) looking into
the camera lens - YouTube.com/JoseffaTrip

Several people in front of the camera

One of the scariest things to do? Be on camera. One of the best ways to take away nerves? Be on camera *together.*

During my video workshops, if I see people being very nervous in front of the camera, I often encourage people to be on camera together. It's a great way to loosen up a bit. Talking with two or three people is a lot different than talking alone. If you're interviewing coworkers, for example, and they're stumbling through their nerves, try to put two people in front of the camera at the same time. You often see the dynamics change in an instant.

But putting several people in front of a camera is not always the right solution. Every person who's visible on the screen needs to be there for a reason; it needs to make sense.

I've interviewed many people, and for most interviews I'm not on the screen. You only see the person being interviewed because they carry the story. The only reason for me to be on camera is when I contribute to the conversation. If you don't see me talk, it doesn't make sense for me to be in the shot. So, if you want to put two or more people in front of the camera, think about it: Is it necessary for all people to be on the screen? Do all people have something to add to the conversation?

If it's an equal conversation where both people talk, being on camera together can be a very suitable and much more natural way to record a conversation.

Interviewing Richard MacManus, founder of ReadWriteWeb at SXSW. We're both on screen because we both add to the conversation

Over the shoulder

This is exactly what it sounds like: The camera points over the shoulder of the interviewer. This way of interviewing is a bit more formal, reporter style. Since you can't keep a close eye on the camera when it's behind you, I'd suggest working with a camera operator.

I often use the over-the-shoulder technique when I interview different people in a short amount of time: on the street or at events, for example. But keep in mind that not everyone will agree to a spontaneous interview, and make sure to bring video release forms so people can give official permission to use the footage.

Over-the-shoulder street-interview

NERVES & APPEARING NATURAL

Sweaty hands. Pounding heart. And for the life of me, I couldn't remember my lines. It was my first time being semi-live on TV news. 2008, KDAF-TV, Dallas, Texas. I was standing in front of a huge touchscreen, talking about some amazing fancy new app. I had practiced working with the touchscreen for hours. I knew exactly what I was going to say. But when I walked up to the camera and saw the red light, I felt my confidence slip away. Everything I had practiced was gone.

It's funny how nerves find their way. They got into my body; I simply forgot how to use the touchscreen. They got into my head; I stammered and stuttered through my practiced lines. They got into my voice, turned it an octave higher, and just about closed my throat. It was the longest one-minute segment I've ever recorded. When it was finally done, my boss stormed into the room, looked at me and shouted, "Where is Pelpina?"

I remember that moment vividly, because it was the best question he could have asked. He was so right: while I was there, I wasn't present. I was not focused on the story, on the viewer. I was focused on the red light, and the stupid touchscreen, and I allowed my nerves to take over.

People often say to me: "You're a natural in front of a camera."

As you can see, this is not true. At. All.

Being comfortable in front of a camera did not come naturally to me. You can learn it too.

I'm a shy person by nature, and I used to be incredibly insecure. It took me years, and some really good people around me, to have the courage to be in front of the camera (not just behind the camera and editing).

And once I was finally in front of that camera, I was often so nervous that I would stutter, make up words (often to the amusement of the news anchors), or just completely shut down and say nothing at all.

But here's the good news: Every time I made a mistake, I also learned how to fix it. Every time I faced my fears, I learned how to overcome them. I now see this was just part of the process. Without making mistakes, you don't learn much. And without facing your fears, you don't grow. So, keep making mistakes. Keep facing those fears. It's the only way to learn and grow!

A camera is not natural

I actually hate the words "being a natural," because when you think about it, being in front of a camera is a pretty unnatural thing. You look into a tiny dot, talk to it, laugh at it, and pretend it's a person: pretty weird, right?

When you talk with a real person, you can look them in the eyes, you usually get a smile back, and you can see if someone is listening to what you're saying. You can "read" the person, and you can usually see if your message is coming across.

With a camera, however, you get absolutely no feedback. You have to imagine those eyes and that smile, and you can't read the viewer. So how can you come across "real" and lively? How can you come across like a normal talking person on camera? I'll give you some tips!

"Make a mess and clean it up later, and become a master at not caring what other people think."

Shay Rowbottom, CEO 'Shay Rowbottom Marketing' and LinkedIn Video Influencer

Coming across as natural: tips

Say you make an educational video of about a minute and a half. Please don't try to record the whole minute-and-a-half story in one take. I did this a lot when I started out. The problem with this is, if you mess up one time, you need to redo the whole story. Trust me, it can turn into a long and stressful video shoot.

Divide your story into parts

I've learned to cut my video up in smaller bits. Simply divide your video into smaller parts, and record one part at a time. For example, you can divide an educational video into three tips. Record each tip separately. That way you don't have to do your entire story perfectly in one take, and you can focus on one tip at a time. What's nice about this approach is that you can have a breather between each tip, while you prepare yourself for the next tip!

 Don't try to record your video in one take. Instead, divide your video into smaller parts, and record one at a time.

Convey, don't just talk

Do you want to convey a message? Then make sure that you're not just saying words, but you're trying to make a connection with the viewer.

One of the best ways to do that, in my opinion, is to avoid word-for-word scripts. I've seen it go wrong too many times: People write a detailed script, hang it next to the camera, and then try to read it in a natural way. Trust me: Most people fail terribly at this. Reading scripts naturally doesn't work because we write differently than we speak. In fact, it took me several months to learn how to write the way I personally speak. It's not an easy thing to do!

So how do you then prepare your video, I hear you think?

Not having a script is not the same as not being prepared. As I explained in chapter one, being prepared is the biggest step in video making, and I always work with a video plan. I know my message, I know what I'm going to say, but I don't rehearse the exact words I'll be using. That way, I avoid sounding too scripted. It usually does work to have a few catchwords on paper, though. Compare it to a presentation. You wouldn't write that out and simply read it word-for-word to the group either, right?

Talk to a person

Right before an interview, I often point out the camera, and say: "This is not a camera. It's a person." The camera is just a tool to get a message across; it's the viewer's eye.

So, before you hit record, imagine who you're talking to. Don't think of a vague target audience like, "women between age 30 and 45," but think of a real-life person, someone you know who falls in that target audience. For example, your cousin Julia, or your neighbor Laura. Imagine that person, and think: How would I tell her this? If I were to bump into her on the street now, how would I tell her?

This often helps to calm nerves, and it can also help to get the right tone of voice and use the right words for your target audience.

Film without hurry/pressure

I see it so often: people who hit the record button, and then start talking right away. They feel pressure to hurry, because as soon as they hit record, they see the seconds ticking by.

 When you hit the record button, don't start talking immediately. Allow yourself to breathe. Give yourself some space to think.

It's good to be aware of this, and to try to remove this pressure to hurry during the video shoot. When you hit the record button, don't start talking immediately. Allow yourself to breathe. Give yourself some space to think: Who are you talking to? What do they need to know?

During interviews, be aware that your energy and attitude can help create the atmosphere in the air. Even if you only have ten minutes to get a short quote from the mayor, don't put that pressure on the mayor.

Always try stay calm, believe me: It will give you much better interviews and vlogs. A few ways to do this:
- Don't tell people you only have x minutes for this video shoot.

- Do tell people you'll stay until it's perfect, even if it takes ten takes.
- Do tell people you can edit out any mistakes, and you'll only leave the good parts.

This can help take away pressure people might be feeling. And when someone feels comfortable in front of the camera, video shoots usually go a lot faster!

My camera routine

Whenever I shoot a vlog or educational video by myself, I always have a certain routine:
- I prepare a video plan, and have a goal for every clip.
- If I feel stressed, I allow myself to calm down by breathing long and slow breaths. If I feel tired, I try to get energized by doing jumping jacks.
- Before I hit record, I think: Who am I talking to? What do I want him/her to know?
- When I hit record, I take a few seconds. I breathe, look into the camera (person!), and start with a smile.
- If I misspeak, I restart the sentence and keep going. No need to stop recording, I can edit the mistake out afterwards.
- I try to remain calm until the last second of the last sentence. Then I smile, hold the smile for two seconds, and stop recording.

At first, it can feel a bit forced to start and end with a smile. But I say: Give it a try. You'll notice that when your video starts with a smile, it'll start off with a warm, good first impression!

Always start and end with a smile

One at a time

I don't know a lot of people who like to watch videos of themselves. It can be very difficult and just downright humiliating to see yourself stumble across a video segment. That's because normally you don't see yourself talking, and you're often hardest on yourself. You see everything that's wrong with you, from the way your voice sounds, to the size of your forehead, to how fast you blink.

Once you start making a lot of videos, it can be very helpful, though, to analyze yourself, to hear your voice, and see your expression, how you hold your hands, and perhaps nervous tics.

You first need to be aware of something before you can improve it, right?

Say, when you watch your videos, you notice that you're not smiling, you're constantly hopping from one foot to the other, and your right hand keeps fiddling with your jacket.

Instead of trying to tackle these three problems all at once, my advice is to work on one at a time.

First, start off with working on your smile. For the next couple of videos, focus on smiling more. At first, it might feel fake or strange to force a smile. Keep practicing until the smiling becomes a new habit, part of your routine. Give yourself some time. You can learn a new habit in just one or two videos, but it could also take seven!

Once you've practiced this new habit and it's become a part of your routine, you move on to the next: standing still.

 Don't be too harsh on yourself, don't tackle too many problems at the same time. Focus on improving one skill.

What I've learned in coaching others to be more comfortable in front of the camera is that you don't want to tackle too many problems at the same time. If you focus on improving one skill, it becomes easier to handle. And eventually, it's all about learning new habits and making them a part of your routine.

Learning to be comfortable, calm, and truly yourself in front of a camera: that's what it's about. And because that does not come naturally to most people, including me, give yourself some time and space to work on this. One at a time. You've got this!

INTERVIEW TIPS: HOW TO GET GREAT QUOTES

I have done many interviews, and I've made a lot of mistakes, especially in the first few years. My first interviews were way too long. I hardly listened to the answers, and I just worked my way down a list of questions. I also had no clue how to calm someone who was nervous for an interview.

I could write a whole separate book on interviewing, but let's just start off with a few tips!

Prepare well

Send or discuss a briefing beforehand, with a clear expectation. ("I am looking for one short quote of 10-15 seconds.") You can add a few sample questions. You can, of course, use these sample questions during the interview as a warmup, but keep the real questions for during the interview, to ensure spontaneous answers.

Warm up

Always assume that the person who is being interviewed needs to warm up a bit first. You can do this by asking a few simple "low-ball" questions. For example, ask for an introduction, or use the questions from the briefing. The length of the warmup differs per person; that's something you'll have to sense during the interview. Once the person is warmed up, you can ask the real questions, so that you get the natural answers.

Communication team at ROC Tilburg
interviewing with smartphone

Start a normal conversation

Don't talk about the production and technical side of the interview too much. When you're setting up the camera and testing the audio, don't always name everything that's happening. The person you're interviewing will only get more nervous when you say you're going to put the camera a little closer, or if you count down before you hit record.

Just try to have a natural conversation, and try to flow into the interview.

Listen, Listen, Listen

The best interviewers don't ask questions; they listen. Don't go through the list of questions one by one. Always listen to the person you're having a conversation with. If you listen carefully, you can often come up with much more interesting questions than you had planned, the interview will go a lot deeper, and you will eventually come back with nicer quotes.

 If you get someone to laugh for a moment, even if it is just a small smile, it allows the person to loosen up a little bit.

Use humor

Don't be afraid to use humor, even during business interviews. When I'm setting up the lights, for example, I sometimes mention that it looks as if the other person is at the dentist under those bright lights, and that this interview will hopefully be a little less painful. Also, don't be afraid to occasionally use a joke during the interview, or to say something spontaneous. If you get someone to laugh for a moment, even if it is just a small smile, it allows the person to loosen up a little bit.

Stop and take a break

Do you notice that it's not working? That the person you're interviewing is still super nervous and isn't able to get a word out of their mouth?

Stop what you're doing.

Don't keep pushing. Take a quick break and do something completely different. Talk about a different subject, or let them take a quick walk around the block. Something that also helps is to sit next to the person during that break. You step out of your role as interviewer/camera person and sit next to them as a person. A short break can often be very helpful; sometimes you only need a couple of minutes, but it can be exactly what you need for a much more relaxed interview!

Keep going!

I have trained hundreds of companies in making videos, and almost everyone makes the same mistake in the beginning: stopping the camera too often and too quickly.

For all types of videos (vlog, interview, presentation, etc.), keep going! If someone misspeaks for a moment, do not stop the camera immediately to talk about the mistake. Keep recording and let the person start again with that specific sentence. Stopping the camera repeatedly increases the chance that the person in front of the camera will get out of the "flow" of the story. This also applies to you: If you film yourself and you make a mistake, resume the sentence and just keep going! You can simply cut out that part in the edit. You've got this!

FILM &
EDIT FASTER

CHAPTER FOUR

*Watch this video by simply holding your
smartphone camera towards the QR code*

FILMING FASTER

Making a video takes a lot of time. Right? You need to think of a good idea, storyboards need to be made, scripts need to be approved, and then everything needs to be filmed at different locations, and let's not even start talking about editing: That takes the longest!

Sure, making videos can definitely take a lot of time.

Through the years, however, I have tested amazing new tools and apps. I have learned to film and edit much faster with less equipment, and the "fast and simple" videos I make now generate a lot more reach than the complicated productions I made in the past. I have learned to switch to newer, faster systems and really follow the principle of "less is more."

The "fast and simple" videos I make now generate a lot more reach than the complicated productions I made in the past.

Let me give you an example. When I started making videos for Frankwatching, I did it the way I used to do it in my video/podcast time. I shot an interview with four cameras and three lights, and I edited for hours and hours on Adobe Premiere Pro. I didn't mind, though; it was just the way to produce videos at the time. Besides, at the time we were the only Dutch channel to post a weekly business video on YouTube. So I'm very proud of those productions. But boy, have things changed in just a few years!

Nowadays, I mainly use my phone to make videos for Frankwatching in an hour or two. I went from four cameras and three lights to one smartphone and a window. I use an app that automatically captions my videos and makes them square, and can publish the video straight from my phone. What a world of difference with how I used to do things in 2011!

Hero videos vs home videos

Of course, there is a difference in production quality and control over settings when you compare smartphones to professional cameras. In 2011, I shot with a good DSLR camera, Sennheiser microphones, and nice softboxes, and my professional editing program gave me the ability to adjust almost everything.

Now when I shoot with my phone, I have less control over the depth of field or colors, and I have fewer editing options.

What I have come to learn, though, is that having fewer options doesn't necessarily mean it's less of a video. It simply means you work with what you've got, and usually that speeds up the filming and editing process tremendously. I can easily get lost for hours in all the amazing options of Final Cut Pro and Adobe Premiere Pro. But when you're making a quick product unboxing, having fewer editing options can actually be a relief. Fewer options means fewer things to sort out.

But the biggest reason I've started to shed equipment is the actual results. I generate a lot more reach and interaction with the simple videos versus the long, well-produced videos. I have never had as much reach (and business!) as I have with my smartphone videos on LinkedIn.

So, to simplify things, I divide business videos in two camps: hero videos and home videos.

Hero videos

The hero videos are the well-produced storytelling videos with beautiful shots, where lines, colors, and composition are all in perfect harmony. These are the videos on your homepage, or the LinkedIn company page, the type of videos you might want to outsource to a professional if you don't have a lot of experience with video.

Home videos

The home videos, on the other hand, are the videos that don't require perfect production to let the message come across. They're about the people within the company (vlogs and behind the scenes), answering questions (Q&As), and showing processes or products (product reviews/product unboxings). With the right knowledge and knowhow, you can often make these inhouse, with a vlog camera or simply with your smartphone.

Whenever I help a company with a video strategy, that's one of the first things I explain. Because all this actually comes back to the 3 Ps: People, Platform, Purpose (chapter one). Depending on who you want to reach, and on what platform, and with what goal, you decide the shape of the video. With that you also have the choice to go for a more complex production or a simple video.

Film different videos in one shoot

Want a handy rule of thumb for making videos fast and efficiently? Never make just one video. If you already have the equipment in place, are in the right location with good light and audio, and have the right person in front of the camera, you might as well record multiple videos.

Suppose you make a video with a colleague sharing a bunch of tips about a new installation. Would you be able to make different videos about this? Perhaps every tip can be a separate video, so you can make three or maybe even five videos. Now, instead of one video out of one shoot, you get a video series out of one shoot, and plenty of content for the future! This also applies to interviews. If you already have an appointment and the person in front of the camera, try to get multiple videos from that one interview instead of just one video.

I do this all the time. Even when I make simple how-to videos for my social channels, I never record just one video, but always at least three. I usually have several shirts ready for each video (otherwise viewers will ask why I'm wearing the same thing. Really! This way I have several videos from just one video shoot.

Richard Moore is king of repurposing video content. Richard has been running a live one-hour Q&A every Monday for three years. He livestreams to three different platforms at the same time. Afterwards, the one-hour Q&A gets broken down into quotes, short videos, and mini articles, which are released throughout the week. So, essentially, with just a one-hour session, he has video content for the rest of the week!

"It's essential to understand that you need to be efficient and frequent with production of content. The way to do that is to repurpose from pillar content. That's where I keep myself efficient, so I can focus on the things that matter, like the relationships and building the business."

Richard Moore, founder of
Entrepreneur Business Live Events

Delete footage while you're filming

For me, the editing process actually already starts during recording. If I make several closeup shots of a product and there's one that I think is the nicest, I immediately delete the other ones. Sometimes I'll record an intro three times, choose which I like best, and immediately delete the other two takes.

Yes, this can be a bit scary, because it's a nice feeling to know that you still have backups. But believe me, I became way more rigorous when I noticed how much time it saves me to delete clips during the video shoot. Once you're about to edit, you don't have to scroll through all the different clips (12 takes that look exactly the same!) and pick out the best ones. If you delete during the video shoot, you have all the right clips ready to go, and you simply need to put them together.

Work with a video format

Remember that piecing a puzzle together works best when you have thought of a plan beforehand. That is the foundation. We already talked about this extensively in chapter one. Divide your video up into several parts (for example, intro, video bumper, quotes, outro), and also know approximately how long each part will take. This way, you can film and edit with more focus.

A format is a video plan for a series of videos. It's a basic mold, a template you can use for all the videos in a series. I love to brainstorm about creative, efficient video formats and have helped many companies with effective social video formats. On the next page, you will find two examples of video formats for the Dutch Red Cross I helped create.

Red Cross: Volunteers Stories

A format in which a Red Cross volunteer shares a story in two minutes. Caregiver Erik, for example, talks about what he did after the attack on the Dutch queen in 2009.

The format:
- Two-minute video
- Start with a powerful quote
- Followed by title of video and music
- Followed by the story in short quotes
- Fill up with B-roll
- End with the Red Cross logo and music

Red Cross: Street Talk

"Street talk" is also a video format for the Dutch Red Cross, but completely different. It's a series of short interviews with people on the street, asking questions like, "Are you well prepared for a flood?" and "What is an AED?"

The format:
- 1.5- to two-minute video
- Short introduction to the topic by an expert
- Followed by short answers from interviews
- Followed by deeper explanation by an expert
- End with the Red Cross logo and music

Once you have come up with the format, you know exactly what to focus on when you're out on the video shoot. For the second format, for example, you need short street-

VIDEO SMART

interviews with a variation in answers, an intro of the topic, and an explanation of the topic. Because you've already decided the length of the video, you also know the length for each clip: five to ten seconds per quote. That allows you to focus during interviews, and helps get shorter and more-specific quotes during filming. This makes filming a lot easier, and the editing process much faster.

LinkedIn Business Tips

And then the format for my business vlogs on LinkedIn. I make a lot of knowledge videos: simple educational videos in which I talk about a video trend or cool new editing app. The videos are usually a few minutes in length.

The format:
- Two- to three-minute video
- Short teaser to get the attention
- Bumper of a few seconds with branding
- Followed by an explanation with CTA interwoven
- End with website/CTA/music

Because I know exactly what the format looks like, I'm able to shoot several videos back to back with a clear focus. For each video I need a teaser, the content (usually divided into steps that I need to record separately), and a good ending.

Making a video plan (see chapter one) and applying it to a series of videos not only allows you to shoot several videos back to back, you can also work with more focus, which speeds up the filming and editing process!

Brian Schulman, founder & CEO of Voice Your Vibe, created "Shout Out Saturday," a highly successful weekly video series on LinkedIn

Start with one pilot

Once you have thought of a good video format, shooting and editing a bunch of videos right after each other is the fastest. But at the very beginning, when you're starting with the first video of a series, my advice is to start with one pilot, one example video.

That's because you can learn a lot from shooting and editing that first video. Perhaps you find out that the setting doesn't fully match what you had in mind. Or maybe the sound logo is too long. Or the call to action needs to be put at the start of the video.

As you can imagine, it's a lot more work to have to re-edit three, four, or 14 videos than to get the first video right and then use that one as an example.

That's why I always start with one pilot when launching a new video series. We take our time to shoot the pilot, to edit it, and then we extensively discuss and evaluate the video. Only after the whole team has given its feedback on the first video do we finish the rest of the series.

The foundation needs to be good, and once it is, you can shoot and edit the rest of the series back to back!

EDITING FASTER

Before we dive into editing, I want to emphasize that editing efficiently starts with good preparation. When you work with a clear video plan/video format, editing is made a lot easier. You want to prevent having an editor go through a 45-minute interview, take out useful bits, and magically transform it into a one-minute video. You ideally want to deliver the right short quotes, so the editing process is really as simple as putting the quotes in order.

Remember to start deleting unneeded footage during the video shoot. That way you don't have to go through 30 clips that all look the same.

Work with an editing template

I also always advise to work with an editing template. Especially for video series, having a template can save a lot of time. An editing template is a standardization of the design of your video. Think about:

- Bumper for the series: a few seconds of video for branding and recognizability
- Sound logo: your company logo, perhaps animated, with sound or music
- Lower thirds: text bar at the bottom of the screen in the style of the company
- Titles: fullscreen or split-screen title screen(s)
- Transparent logo at the top or bottom of the screen
- End screen with logo/call to action
- Music track (See tips in chapter two)

You can standardize and develop the above elements for a whole series of videos. This way, you don't need to search for music for each video or think about where you want to place the logo; there's no need to reinvent the wheel.

Become a faster editor

When I was in my early twenties, I was convinced that I would later become a film or video editor. I thought (and still think) that editing is fantastic: it's a creative process in which you are able to puzzle a bunch of pieces together.

I have worked with a bunch of different editing software. I started with Avid on TV news, transferred over to Adobe

Premiere Pro, and a few years later I used Final Cut Pro. I knew all the software inside out, and I still love to edit on my laptop and get lost in Final Cut Pro for hours.

But for most of my *home productions*, you won't find me editing with professional editing software anymore. I now simply edit on my phone. There are a ton of video-editing apps that speed up the video-editing process, and also, I can literally edit a video anywhere!

This book is not a manual with detailed steps on how to edit in the coolest video editing apps because the apps change fast (if you're looking for extensive app tutorials, check my online academy on pelpina.com). But I do want to give you a good foundation on how to edit fast.

I have edited thousands of videos and have made a lot of mistakes. The way I used to work, especially in the first couple of years, was very inefficient, which caused me to edit for hours (sometimes even days). To help you prevent this, here are some standard editing steps for basically every video.

Step 1. Delete during the video shoot

You saw this tip earlier in this chapter. Editing, for me, starts during recording. It can be frustrating to have to go over 16 videos that look the same: Which one was the right clip again? A more efficient way is to start deleting clips you know you won't use during the video shoot. So did you just record ten different clips and was take #7 the best? Do yourself a favor and delete the other nine!

*Avoid having too many similar videos in your camera roll.
Delete during the shoot, so you don't have to go through
many (very similar) clips during the edit*

Step 2. Look at what you have

The first thing I always do before I start editing is scroll
through all my footage and look through everything that I
have. If it is an extensive shoot, with different interviews,
for example, I make notes: a short list with quotes and their
corresponding time frames, for example.

I do the same for B-roll: Which shots are the prettiest?
Which images fit the quotes? You can often get a good
sense of the final video by going through and screening all

the footage. At this point, puzzling everything together probably has already started in your mind.

While going through the footage, again you can delete clips you won't need. This way the selection of usable clips gets smaller and smaller, which makes the eventual editing process faster.

Don't just look at the visuals, but also check the quality of the audio. This way, you avoid ending up with a good-looking clip with bad audio. Using good quality over the ear headphones can help with this, especially when you're not in a quiet room.

You can also already cut up the quotes or fill shots, straight from your camera roll. On most phones, you simply tap "edit" to change the start and end point, or to rotate the video.

Do the first fast edits straight from your camera roll. Tap "edit" to change the duration, orientation and colors

Step 3. Edit the quotes

Most videos have a person, or multiple people as the foundation of a video. This can be someone being interviewed, a person sharing their knowledge in front of a camera, or a voiceover. The people are usually the basis of the content of the video. That's why I always start with finding the right quotes.

In step two, the screening, you usually already have a good idea of which quotes or which clips work well. In this step you will apply that. Cut the clips shorter to the exact right quotes. Put them in the right order. This can be a bit of a puzzle, but if you already had a clear video plan and have done the screening, this step should not take too long.

Step 4. Continue with fill shots

Once you've put in the voiceover, interview quotes, or vlog bits, you also know which fill shots, or B-roll, would match what quote. We'll apply the "say-dog-see dog" principle. Simply select the right B-roll and place it over or between the quotes. For example, when a vlogger is talking about a fire truck, you put an image of a fire truck over or after the quote.

Step 5. Graphics and text

This is usually seen as the "fun" part of the video: adding transitions, texts, sounds, etc. But make no mistake: The right graphics and subtitles can really be the deciding factor about whether people will click on your video. So, I actually see this as crucial decoration to your video: The right arrows, banners, and titles can make your video interesting to watch. On top of that, most social videos are watched without audio, so always make sure that people are able to follow your video without audio by using captions or graphics.

LinkedIn influencer and video expert Shay Rowbottom uses captions, graphics, and text to optimize her videos

You want to save captioning as the very last step. It can be frustrating to have the whole video captioned and to get feedback that one quote needs to be taken out and one needs to be added. It's better to have the video finished, sent in for feedback, and then start with the transitions, graphics, titles, and captions (more about captions in a bit!). As a side note, I usually think this is one of the most fun parts of editing, so this way you save the best for last!

EDITING APPS & SOFTWARE

Using the best tools, software and apps can save you a lot of time during the edit-process. I'm always trying out new video apps, and so my short list of go-to apps changes constantly. Check out my website pelpina.com and LinkedIn profile to keep up to date with the apps I'm currently using.

Video editing apps

As I mentioned before, I edit most of my videos on my phone. One of the main things I've learned is that if you have no or little editing experience, start with simple videos, a good plan and an intuitive video editing app or software.

I love editing on my phone: I don't need to upload my footage to my laptop, and I can do everything on one device: film, edit, and publish.

I usually use several apps to edit one video. So, I start editing in iMovie, for example, and finish up my edit in MixCaptions.

For a current list of apps with extensive video tutorials, check out my eCourses at pelpina.com. On the next pages you can find several apps I have used extensively for quite some time.

Quik (free, Android & iPhone)

A nice app that does
what it says it does: It
makes a video quickly.
Simply select a few
videos and pictures, and
Quik automatically edits
it for you. You can
choose from more than
ten themes to give your
video a certain look and
feel, add text and change
the order of the clips, and
within a couple of
minutes you've got a fun
video. For videos with a
business purpose,
Quik is especially
useful to create fast

impression videos, event videos, or short vlogs. Calmer
themes include "Raw," "Grammy," and "Lapse." When
you're editing a quote, you can adjust the length by tapping
the scissors "trim," and change the audio to "boost." And
it's also important to know that it's possible to turn off the
Quik logo!

The main downside of this app: it doesn't allow you to
work in layers (you can't put a video over a video, or a logo
over your entire video, for example). It's a slide-show with
a combination of pictures and videos. This app is also great
for vacation and sports videos – I use this app for videos of
my family and business!

iMovie (free, iPhone)

A wonderful app to edit videos fast. Quickly trim, rotate, and crop your videos. iMovie is incredibly intuitive, and it also lets you edit with (limited) layers: you can place a video over a video – for example, you can put fill shots over an interview. iMovie also lets you work with green-screen, add text and music to your video, change the volume of a clip, and add effects. I definitely recommend this app for beginners.

Kinemaster (subscription, Android & iPhone)

An extensive app that allows you to work with layers: video over video, on top of that a logo, and on top of that text, for example. Kinemaster has a ton of options like animations, title screens, and fonts; you can even use keying for when you're in front of a greenscreen and want to change the background. It's also possible to record a voiceover within the app. Kinemaster offers a ton of audio-editing options, such an audio envelope (which allows you to change the volume with audio points throughout the

clip). The app also has an extensive library with paid and free add-ons, such as different fonts, title screens and themes. I recommend Kinemaster when you want to regularly edit company videos and need control over the look and feel. It's an intuitive app with a ton of options!

The app is free to use with the Kinemaster logo visible; to lose the logo you have to subscribe.
Are you looking for a free app with similar options and do you have an iPhone? Then check out the app *Cute Cut Pro*. It works in a similar way, just a bit less intuitive and with fewer options than Kinemaster.

BigVu (subsription, Android & iPhone)

An app developed specifically to create business videos on your smartphone! You can record videos fast with the app's intuitive teleprompter tool (just remember to look into the camera lens).

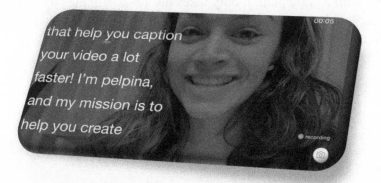

The app lets you add titles, a logo, music, and an intro and outro. If you record in front of a green screen, you can change the background with BigVu.

Premium users can also easily add visuals in the videos, such as photos, videos and tweets. And BigVu can also automatically caption your video in most languages. It even lets you change the style accentuate certain words. Definitely a great app/system to create professional videos with your smartphone. I highly recommend this app if you're a serious video creator and want to streamline a lot of video productions!

Clips (free, iPhone)

An app that automatically captions your videos while you're recording live. You can also caption B-roll (pictures and videos). Clips has a library with fun animated title screens and lots of music. For iPhones 10 and up, Clips also offers "scenes": animated 3D backgrounds. It's especially useful for short tip videos or short vlogs.

A good video plan is crucial if you're using this app. I use Clips often to quickly make a tip-video for LinkedIn, for example.
And with a good plan, it only takes me 15-20 minutes to make a video with captions, different clips, B-roll/pictures, and animated intro/outro screens!

Inshot (free, iPhone/Android)

This is my favorite app to add graphics and text to my
videos. This app lets you
fully control text: font,
color, size, duration, and
even animation. You can
also add pictures (or a
logo) from your camera
roll. Another reason this
app is a huge favorite: it
lets you crop the video to
another size
(vertical, square,
5:4, etc.), and even lets you
create fun banners at the
top and bottom of your
video.

After an initial edit in
Clips/iMovie/Kinemaster, I usually export my video to
finish up the edit in InShot. Pro tip: in the free version, you
can click on the InShot logo to remove it!

Vormats (subscription, Android & iPhone)

A video app specifically developed for business videos.
This app is an all-in-one: it helps you with a video plan and
thinks along with every take. Vormats also lets you put in
B-roll and a logo, and is even able to caption the video. I
recommend Vormats for company videos, vlogs,
explainers, product videos, etc.

Autocap (Android)

This app also automatically captions your videos. The main difference with Clips is that this app lets you caption prerecorded videos. You can put in videos from your library, and Autocap will caption them for you. You can then change the spelling or the words, and export your video. I definitely recommend this app to caption your videos fast!

 For current useful video apps (with video tutorials), check my online academy at pelpina.com.

Editing software

If you prefer working on a laptop or desktop, you can also use editing software. I've trained many professionals in editing, and my main tip is: find intuitive, easy to use software that works for you. I recommend downloading a trial (usually valid for 30 days) to see if you like the software. If you want to edit on a computer or laptop, instead of on your phone, here are few options:

iMovie

This free software for Mac is especially nice for beginning editors. You're able to edit in layers (video over video), add titles, place transitions between clips, and even key (removing one color, for example, for a greenscreen). But title options, graphics, and working in layers are pretty limited, so if you're looking for more control, check out one of the following options.

Camtasia

An intuitive editing program for Windows and Mac, Camtasia allows you to work with unlimited layers and has a library with all kinds of title screens, graphics/ icons, music, and low-threshold animation options. On top of that, it has a captioning tool that allows you to basically type along with the video. This is a favorite in most of my video editing workshops.

Add captions fast with Camtasia's caption tool

Final Cut Pro

The professional video editing program for Mac with a one-time payment. I switched to Final Cut Pro because it allows you to synchronize different camera angles with one click of a button. It's a pretty intuitive program, and it also has a ton of pro options, such as color correction, 360-

degree video editing, video stabilization, and HDR (High Dynamic Range) support.

Adobe Premiere Pro

The professional video editing program from Adobe (with subscription) that works on Windows and Macs. This is a program for advanced editors, perfect if you're used to editing in layers and want to take your video editing to the next level. It has extensive options for title editing, audio editing, and the ability to further edit the video in Adobe After Effects.

DaVinci Resolve

Free video-editing software that also allows you to work in layers. DaVinci Resolve has a library with title screens, filters, and effects, and even a color-correction tool and audio editor. All of these options are free in this version. DaVinci Resolve Studio is the paid model, with even more options like 3D tools and HDR grading, and sharing the edit project with multiple people.

Free editing software DaVinci Resolve

Outsourcing editing

If editing inhouse is not an option, and you have a decent
budget, you can outsource the editing process. In the past
couple of years, new and quite innovative ways to
outsource video editing have come about. You can send
your footage to inhousefilming.com, Viddedit.com, and
Vidchops.com, and they will edit it professionally. Or, find
a local editor who understands the style you have in mind.
That way, you can keep the filming process inhouse, while
you're also assured of a professionally edited video.

CAPTIONS & SUBTITLES

More than 80% of all videos on social networks are
watched without audio. So, it is very important that the
video is understandable without the audio on.
My advice is to caption every video you put on social
media, whether that is through closed captions or open
captions.

Closed captions can be turned on or off by the viewers.
They're basically a separate layer to a video. Closed
captions are uploaded as a separate text file. They can be
useful if you want to give the viewer the option to turn
captions on or off and pick from different languages.

Open captions are burned into the video; they cannot be
turned off by the viewers. One huge advantage of open
captions is that these don't require special functionality for
media players or platforms, and you don't have to upload a
separate file along with your video. If you choose for open

captions, you can decide on the style of the captions (font, size, and positioning).

Captions are the final step

Whether you can turn the captions on or off, whether they're white, black, purple, or have a yellow border, the fact is that captions are a must. It's a step you have to take, and it should be the final step in the production process.

After the video has been completely edited (including feedback rounds from everyone on the team), and completely approved, it's time to caption.

It can take a while to caption a video. The last thing you want to receive after captioning is further feedback on the content of the video ("quote A needs to be replaced with something else"). You then not only have to re-edit the content, but also the captions. So, save the captions for last!

Tools to make captioning faster

Captioning videos can be time-consuming. Thankfully, however, there are all kinds of tools and apps to speed up the caption process. The world of captioning tools and techniques is constantly moving. We now live in a world where speech recognition is integrated on almost every phone, and software and apps can transcribe audio.

I believe this will develop enormously in the coming years, and in a few years, we won't have to caption our own videos anymore. Smart software, TVs, and phones will be able to recognize what is being spoken.

And something that I'm already looking forward to are devices that, based on personal information or location, know which language needs to be used for the subtitles. So, say you're speaking Dutch in the video. That video will be automatically captioned in French when seen in France, or to Urdu in Pakistan.

Unfortunately, we're not there yet; but there are a ton of useful services, cool apps, and professional software that can make captioning faster and easier.

Next, I'll dive into four different ways to caption your videos: typing captions yourself, using a transcribe function, automated captions, and captioning services.

Typing captions

Do you have a short video, and don't mind typing the captions? I recommend using the apps VLLO or Inshot to caption the video yourself. In VLLO, for example, you select the caption tool and simply type out every sentence within the app.

Transcribe function

Some apps and websites transcribe your finished video for you. The technology basically "listens" to your video and automatically generates your script with timecodes for you. On the next pages you will find a few options.

YouTube

Have you discovered YouTube's transcribe function? YouTube automatically generates captions for each uploaded video. This means that for each video (also for the ones that are on private), you can download a ready-made captions file – a script with timecodes.

Automatic captioning on YouTube

All you have to do is upload your video, find it in your YouTube Studio, and click on CC (Closed Captions). You will then find the automatic script YouTube has created, along with the right timing. Pretty amazing! You can change the text/periods/capital letters, if you want. After that, you can download the captions file (in SRT or VTT format), which you can then upload alongside your video on Facebook or LinkedIn, for example, or import the file in a professional editing program.

Autocap (Android)

Autocap allows you to
caption previously recorded
clips, just like YouTube
does, but straight from your
phone. Simply upload a
video in the app, and
Autocap automatically
captions it for you. You
don't need to record from
the app, which is the case
with Clips. Autocap also
lets you choose from
different font styles, and it's
also possible to edit the
captions afterwards.

It can be a bit tedious to get the timing of the words
completely right, but that's mainly if you start looking at
milliseconds (and are a perfectionist like I am!).

Mixcaptions (iPhone)

Upload your video to MixCaptions, and the app
automatically captions your video. This is one of my
favorite apps, it saves me a ton of time!
After I finish editing my video (in iMovie or InShot for
example), I upload the video to MixCaptions.
Simply select the spoken language, and the app will
transcribe the video. You can pick from different caption
styles, and you can also edit the captions afterwards.
MixCaptions lets you add your logo (paid option), and you
can also export your video in different sizes. I use

MixCaptions for almost all videos I post on LinkedIn. The app is free if you don't mind the Mixcaptions watermark, otherwise you pay per video. Since my videos are pretty short (less than three minutes usually), I pay less than a Euro for every video. I highly recommend this app.

BigVu

BigVu lets you read a script with its intuitive teleprompter function, trim clips and add logo/ intro/outro, and premium users can also add burned-in captions to videos. BigVu can either use your script, or it can transcribe your video in most languages. You can edit the words and change the caption style (even let some words stand out in different colors!). BigVu is a great option for companies that regularly want to caption videos, in their own style, without hassle!

Captions CC

An app that transcribes your videos in a similar way as Autocap, with the difference that Captions CC currently only works on iPhones. You can change the words in the script and adjust the timecodes. At the time that I'm writing this book, this app is not very intuitive, but nevertheless, it's one of the first apps with a transcribe function.

Vormats

This app is being developed while I'm writing this book. I've been able to access a beta version and I'm very impressed. This app is specifically developed to make business videos. Vormats gives you the option to caption your video with an SRT file, which you can then upload along with your video on Facebook, LinkedIn, or YouTube. Definitely an app to watch!

Automatic captions during recording

Some apps generate the captions for you while you're recording. The captions appear automatically in your video, live as you speak.

Clips (iPhone)

Clips is a very intuitive app that captions your videos automatically. While you're talking, the words you say appear on the screen, thanks to speech recognition.

To be able to get captions on the video, you need to record in the app, and you can choose from many different languages. After you've recorded, you can change the words in the captions by tapping "text." Clips offers many different caption styles. Besides automatic captions, this app also has nice graphics, effects, and text animations. Videos are automatically made square.

The biggest downside is that it's not easy to cut out a small piece of a clip – during interviews, for example. Having a good video plan is a must while using this app. Clips is my go-to app for educational videos on LinkedIn. I recommend it for short videos with one person talking.

Clipomatic (iPhone)

A similar app to Clips, with the main difference being that Clipomatic records vertically (the standard in Clips is square). Clipomatic is perfect for Instagram Stories. After recording, you're able to edit the words, just like in Clips, and you can choose from 40 different languages.

Caption services

Do you not want to spend time on uploading your videos and editing the captions manually? There are several apps and websites you can use that make this process a lot easier.

Amberscript.com

Send your video to Amberscript, and you will receive a subtitle file in your inbox, for a bit over a dollar per minute of video (depending on the type of service).

Rev.com

Get a transcript for a dollar per minute of video. I have had good experiences with Rev.com; I always receive my captions in my inbox within a few hours. Rev.com also offers to translate your captions, which can be useful for international companies.

Splasheo.com

Splasheo makes sure your video is ready for upload on
social media; it doesn't get any simpler than this. It's a
fantastic tool for open captions – subtitles that are burned in
the video. Simply send your video to Splasheo, and then
determine the layout: Do you want a square version of your
video?
What color do you want the bars to be? Do you need text in
the bars? You will receive different versions of your video
in your inbox within 24 hours. I love the catchy layout
(colorful banners) and the captions Splasheo offers.
Splasheo works with various subscriptions. For more,
check www.splasheo.com/pelpina.

Video banners, text and captions made with Splasheo.com

PUBLISHING VIDEOS

CHAPTER 5

Watch this video by simply holding your smartphone camera towards the QR code

Yes, your video is finished! You created a plan, shot the video, edited it, and now it's ready to share with your target audience. But hold on a second before you press "publish." In this chapter, I focus on a publishing plan: When should you post your video? What should you pay attention to when posting a video on LinkedIn? And how do you optimize your video for YouTube? If you think about the publication beforehand and plan it out, your results could be a whole lot different than if you just post it without preparation.

START WITH A GOAL

Your video is finally finished, and you can't wait to post it online. I understand you want to share it with the world, but let's focus first. Let's go back to your initial goal. Before you started filming, you (should have) made a video plan. What was your plan? You are going to put that into practice now!

Remember the 3 Ps: People, Platform, Purpose. You start with your ideal viewer, adjust your video to the platform, and always have the final purpose in mind: What should your viewer do, think, or feel while watching your video? Take a moment right now to go back to your 3 Ps: What was your original goal? Where are you going to publish your video? Optimizing a video on YouTube is vastly different from optimizing it on Instagram. That's why we're going to look at a few guidelines to posting videos on different social media platforms.

If you want to publish your video on several platforms, in an ideal world you would optimize your video differently for each platform. Unfortunately, most of us don't have the time and resources to create three or four different versions of one video. That's why my advice is to optimize your video with just one main platform in mind.

For me, LinkedIn is currently my main platform, so I make my educational videos square, captioned, and around two-three minutes long. This doesn't mean that I only post my videos on

LinkedIn; I also post them on Instagram, YouTube, and Facebook. But my videos have been optimized primarily with LinkedIn in mind.

YOUTUBE OPTIMIZATION GUIDELINES

YouTube is the king of video. Many companies use YouTube to upload videos to embed them on their website or in their newsletter. But YouTube is so much more than a simple means to embed your videos elsewhere. YouTube is a social search engine. It's a place where people go to find answers, to be inspired, and to be entertained. And unlike other platforms, YouTube is where people go to specifically watch videos.

When to post on YouTube

It's quite simple. If you want to be found on YouTube, you have to make videos people are searching for. So, do you know what your target audience is searching for online? What are their main (recurring) questions and problems? What do people search for within your market?

It's with that question in mind that I make videos for Frank-watching – usually on common social media topics such as "How do I delete my Facebook account?" and "How do Snapchat filters work?" For a Dutch railroad company, I made instructional videos on how to use the national public transportation pass: "How do I apply for the transportation pass?" "How does the transportation pass work?" These are "evergreen" videos; they have a long shelf life and will be searched for a long time, which is perfect for YouTube.

If you want to be found on YouTube, you have to make videos on topics people are searching for.

The basic evergreen videos are made to attract new viewers, which is a good foundation for your YouTube channel. Other types of content, such as a weekly vlog, a series with case studies, or product demos, can create a bond between you and your viewers and give them a reason to come back.

When not to post on YouTube

If you use your videos in B2B or education, and you mainly use videos on your website (and don't need to be found on YouTube), YouTube might not be the right platform. Or perhaps you don't want to be on YouTube because it's built on ads and lacks options on branding and customization.

Vimeo might be an interesting alternative; it's clean, less ad-focused, and has the possibility to customize the video player and put passwords on videos.

If you want to go a step further and have full control and rights over your own videos, try an enterprise video platform, or video management system such as Panopto.com, VidGrid.com, or Kaltura.com. These systems give you full control over your business videos – video player look and feel, privacy, analytics, and even interaction (depending on the system, of course). These systems come with a price tag, but depending on your needs, they might be just what you're looking for.

YouTube algorithm

YouTube has been pretty secretive about its algorithm. Fortunately, people like Jeremy Vest, Tim Schmoyer and Justin Briggs have done extensive research into what works on YouTube. Briggs, for example, looked at 3.8 million data points, over 100,000 videos, and 75,000 YouTube channels. He discovered there are basically two ways to optimize your video on YouTube.

- Text that goes along with your video: the title, tags, and description. Make sure you put your keywords (the words your ideal viewer searches for) in the text, preferably in the beginning of your title. The text tells YouTube which searches should match your video. So, optimizing the text is especially essential when the video is first uploaded and fundamental for the optimization of your video.
- Watch time. Once your video has been on YouTube for a day or two, YouTube learns how long people watch your video on average, interact with your video, and what they do after they've watched it. YouTube prefers "long views," videos that are watched for a long time and contribute to long watch sessions on YouTube. YouTube experts like Jeremy Vest and Tim Schmoyer also say that to get your videos higher up in search results, you need to increase your watch time.

Do you want to take a deeper dive into the YouTube algorithm? I definitely recommend following Jeremy Vest, Tim Schmoyer, and Justin Briggs.

"Make videos that answer the questions people are asking on YouTube. Make sure your thumbnails give someone a reason to stop and click on your video, not your competitors."

Jeremy Vest, YouTube Optimization Expert

YouTube Video Optimization Tips

The best way to optimize a YouTube video? A good video! You can optimize a video with text, playlists, and thumbnails, but if you have bad content nobody wants to watch, it's no use. Step one is always good content.

Watch time

In general, videos that attract a long watch time show up higher in search results. So, make sure you not only attract your viewers with an interesting opening, but keep your viewers interested throughout the video. One way to do this is by dividing your video up in different steps: "3 ways to.." "5 hacks for…" or "Top 7…" Formats like this work well, because even if your viewers aren't interested in step 2, for example, they know there's another step coming they might be interested in.

Playlists

Playlists allow you to group videos together and organize them in a logical order. They let the viewers lean back and watch several videos at a time. Jeremy Vest says playlists can increase your search ranking because they help you improve watch time (they auto-play to the next video). That's why it's a good idea to link and share your playlists, not individual videos – because this will help to increase overall watch time.

Jeremy also believes that your channel is valued higher in the YouTube algorithm if you refer people to other channels. One way to do this is by creating a regularly scheduled "Fan video of the week." Say people are making videos about your product. All you have to do is add a video of

13:52

The KEY to Success for LIVE Video Growth in 2020

Live Streaming Pros

someone else to your playlist every week (you don't have to ask permission), and voila! You have a whole new video series!

Optimize thumbnails

You probably recognize this: While you're watching a YouTube video, your eyes wander off to the suggested videos. I've helped a lot of companies with a YouTube strategy, and most often, the majority of the viewers come through suggested videos. This is an important fact, because the best way to optimize for that is by

using a thumbnail that stands out! Instead of picking one of the screen-shots YouTube suggests, make your own thumbnail with Photoshop or Canva. Work with a temp-late, so you don't have to reinvent the wheel with every thumbnail.

Top 5 Marketing Strategies You MUST Steal

Shama Hyder

6:41

5 Marketing Strategies You Should Steal from DTC...

Jeremy Vest suggests that your thumbnail contains a closeup of a face or two faces (with emotion/ expression), high contrast in colors, a few words that describe the video, and perhaps some branding (logo or banners in your company colors).

I personally use Canva.com to create my YouTube thumbnails. It has a ton of free templates and pictures to pick from, and lets you change the words, fonts and colors. Perfect to create a fast thumbnail template!

YouTube Text Optimization Tips

Search engines can't (yet) watch videos, so you need to help YouTube and Google understand what your video is about. The best way to do that is by using text. The obvious text associated with a video: title, description and tags.

Use keywords well and in the right order

Put your most important keywords first in both the title of the video and the tags. Find the best ranking key-words by simply typing a seed keyword in the YouTube search bar: You'll see a list of suggestions. You can also use Google Trends to check the popularity of different keywords (specifically for YouTube as well).

Add links to your website and social channels

If you want viewers to go to a specific website, add it in one of the first two lines in the description so viewers don't have to click on "more." Make sure to include "http://"; otherwise, it doesn't become a clickable link.

LOVE VIDEO CREATORS AND WANT TO GROW ON YOUTUBE? HERE ARE SOME NEXT STEPS!

1) SUBSCRIBE to learn how to grow your YouTube channel!
https://www.youtube.com/channel/UCcB3...

2) FREE GUIDE: "The Secret to Building your YouTube Audience"
https://videocreators.com/the-secret-...

3) BECOME A MEMBER: Access special community perks on our channel and support our trainings
by clicking that Join button! Or, click here: https://www.youtube.com/channel/UCcB3...

4) LET'S CONNECT!
— https://www.facebook.com/videocreators
— https://twitter.com/timschmoyer
— https://instagram.com/timschmoyer
— https://instagram.com/videocreators

Video Description by YouTube expert Tim Schmoyer

Add a standard description/tags

Did you know that you can add a standard description and tags in the upload settings on YouTube? This can save you a ton of time and makes sure each uploaded video is minimally optimized. Of course, you always want to add video-specific info and text. Closed captions and transcripts can also help YouTube and Google index the video and positively impact watch time and user engagement.

You can find much more on closed captions in chapter four.

Optimize the video file

Did you know you can optimize your video file even before you upload it to YouTube?

By changing the file name, tags, and comments that go along with the video file, you help Google and YouTube index your video. Changing the file name from "8364.mp4" to "top smartphone video apps 2020" helps search engines understand the content of the file. You can also go a bit deeper and change the tags and comments within the file.

On a Mac, for example, you simply right-click on your video and go to "get info." You can then not only change the title, but also add tags and a description under "comments."

Optimize the video file by adding tags

LINKEDIN PUBLICATION GUIDELINES

LinkedIn is an interesting platform that has developed enormously in the past few years. LinkedIn has been very effective for my business because it allows me to reach and grow my B2B target audience through vlogs and educational videos. I've posted a ton of videos on LinkedIn, and I can tell you: Visual content is incredibly effective there. Updates with pictures get twice as much response as text updates, and videos receive five times more responses than regular text updates.

"One of the most powerful things about LinkedIn video is its ability to strengthen the process in which entrepreneurs and enterprise qualify their leads. Those who reap the most amount of benefit from LinkedIn video are those who show up daily and don't ask for anything, yet are very articulate on their profile with a call to action that directly speaks to what they want their audience to do."
Sally Illingworth, LinkedIn Video Creator & Strategic Communications Expert

Just like with every network, for an effective strategy on LinkedIn you need to first know your audience. Are you trying to reach professionals in a certain industry or market? CEOs of top companies? Or do you want to network with people with similar professional interests? Then LinkedIn might just be perfect.

When to post on LinkedIn

In order to know when to post on LinkedIn, you need to know how your ideal viewers use LinkedIn.

As you probably know, LinkedIn is mainly used for professional purposes: networking, acquiring knowledge, finding a job/employees/collaborators, and building a personal or company brand.

So the big question remains: How can you be relevant to one of these topics with video? Can you perhaps share professional knowledge that people might find interesting? Do you want to show what you stand for as a potential employee or employer? Or would you like to use personal videos to network?

LinkedIn video algorithm

Some of my videos have reached more than a million views; other videos barely get a few thousand views. Throughout the years of posting videos on LinkedIn, I've learned the algorithm changes constantly. But one thing remains: If you are active on LinkedIn, if you participate in conversations, and if you add content that adds to inter-action and conversations, your content is shown well.

LinkedIn looks at two major aspects:
1. Prioritizing relevant content
2. Promoting interaction

Relevant posts are preferred over new posts in the regular LinkedIn feed. This means that the algorithm mainly looks at how likely it is that a user will like or share a certain post. It tries to predict this by looking at previous activity of the user; which content the user liked, shared, or responded to, and which people the user has had a lot of interaction with.

"After two full years of daily consecutive videos, it has given me a dedicated platform and community. It has also opened incredible doors including a request to  write for *Forbes*, speaking all over the world and representing some of the world's largest brands like WeWork and Adobe as an ambassador."
Goldie Chan, top LinkedIn Content Creator

When posting a video on LinkedIn, it is important to keep two things in mind: relevance and good timing. When does your target audience check LinkedIn? If you're unsure, you can first experiment with different days and times. I also first experimented for a couple of months with my posting times of my knowledge videos. I found that the best time to post for my viewers is at the end of the afternoon (Dutch professionals are almost done with work and American professionals start their day around that time). But the perfect day and time to post differs per audience. So, my advice is to experiment, and find out what the ideal day and time for your audience are.

LinkedIn optimization tips

Make relevant videos for your ideal viewer

This is always step one: Put yourself in the mind of the professional you want to reach and make videos with that ideal viewer in mind. For me, personally, this means videos about practical questions I often receive, such as "How do I caption my video?" or "What are the best apps to edit videos fast?"

Keep it short and start fast

Don't save the essential information until the end of the video, and make sure your video's length is appropriate. LinkedIn recommends that videos include a hook within the first one to two seconds. An internal study by LinkedIn found that videos under 30 seconds reported a 200% lift in view completion rates.

My advice is to also test with longer videos, especially if you want to share knowledge, share a story, or explain a complex idea. The same LinkedIn study found that longer-form content drove as many clicks and views as shorter videos because they help tell a more complex product or brand story.

Design your video for sound off

Up to 85 percent of social media videos are played with no sound. That's why I always use captions on my LinkedIn videos. Make sure to visualize your message (not just show a "talking head," as I explained in chapter two), add graphics and/or words to the video, and use expressive body language.

Diana Nguyen, LinkedIn top voice
and video influencer

Use the right timing

Post the video at a day and time your viewer is online. If you get a lot of interaction once the video has been posted (in the first hour or so), the video will be shown to more people, and ranked higher in the LinkedIn algorithm.

Tag relevant businesses and people

Tag companies or people who are mentioned or have something to do with your video. But be careful to only tag relevant people and businesses. You don't want to be seen as a spammer! The tagged people/companies also get notifications for interactions on your post.

Use relevant hashtags

This is one of the best ways to group videos, since LinkedIn currently doesn't have playlists (yet). Hashtags are perfect for group content and make it easier to find relevant content.

Use a clear description

Don't underestimate the importance of the text that goes along with your video. I usually start with a good headline and try to work with short bullets. Remember to use the right keywords. Several of my videos are found through Google search!

INSTAGRAM PUBLICATION GUIDELINES

Instagram is an enormously fast-growing social network, and it can be very interesting for brands, especially due to high interaction on posts. On average, company pages have ten times higher interaction on Instagram than on Facebook, and 84x more than on Twitter. Seven out of ten hashtags used on Instagram are from a brand or company, and 72% of Instagram users have bought something after they saw a post, story, or advertisement on Instagram. Plus, video consumption on Instagram has increased by more than 80%.

This all sounds very impressive, but as a company, it can be difficult to come up with a good video strategy for Instagram. Time to dive in!

When to post on Instagram

Of course, the first question again is: Do I, as a company, need to be on Instagram? And just like each platform, the same advice also applies here: Are you able to reach your ideal viewer on Instagram? If your ideal viewer is on Instagram, how does he/she communicate, what is he/she looking for, and what are his/her biggest reasons for checking Instagram?

And the question that follows: Can you make content your ideal viewer wants to see on Instagram?

Creating a visual Instagram account around beauty, fashion, food, or technology can be a lot more obvious than around banking, orthodontics, or aerodynamics, for example. If there are no obvious attractive visuals to work with, it might take a bit of creativity to find ways to become visible on Instagram.

Marketing platform Mailchimp, for example, features its mascot Freddie in pictures and videos. Or give your company a face (or faces!) with pictures from team members. Gartner regularly shares fun pictures and videos with the hashtag #lifeatgartner. Another idea is to share interesting quotes from your founder or a team member; Khoros does this well, combining pictures and videos of team members.

Someone I personally follow to keep me up to date on what works on Instagram is Dot Lung. If you don't know where to start, check out her account!

Dot Lung on Instagram

My advice? First check to see if your ideal viewer is active on Instagram, and then which content would fit. What is your ideal viewer looking for? Is it an educational video, a behind-the-scenes video, a short product impression, an FAQ video through IGTV, or perhaps a fun mascot video?

Instagram algorithm

Once you've thought of a fitting video format (check chapter one!), it's good to know how Instagram's algorithm works, so you know how to best optimize your video. Remember, though, the best optimization is always, always, always good content. But let's assume that your content is rocking and is geared to your ideal viewer.

The Instagram algorithm, like every social media platform's, basically focuses on one thing: maximizing the time users spend on the platform. More time equals more advertisements. Accounts that ensure users spend longer on Instagram are appreciated more within the algorithm. And this is where video comes in. Videos can help you get a longer watch time and more interaction on your feed, IGTV, and stories.

Let's zoom in on the algorithm. Where your video is placed within the Instagram feed, its ranking, depends on the factors.

Relationship

If an Instagram user often leaves responses on your posts, has notifications for your account, if you tag each other, or if you DM each other, the algorithm will see a strong relationship. The stronger the relationship, the faster Instagram will show your Instagram post in the user's feed.

Interest

The algorithm decides which posts are important to users based on their past activities. Instagram uses "machine vision technology" for this (recognizing certain pictures) to determine the content and thus to match posts. This is similar to how Facebook and YouTube filter and recommend content. If a certain user has liked a lot of pictures of latte art, the algorithm will put new latte art higher up in the feed in the future.

Time

The Instagram feed is not chronological (new content is not automatically placed on top). Instead, relation and interest are of big influence in the ranking, as I explained above. But don't disregard the timing of your post; even if it's not the most important factor, it still plays a role in ranking. So just like with LinkedIn and YouTube, it's important to know when your audience is on Instagram.

Instagram Stories

The use of Instagram Stories has increased enormously in popularity in the past few years. These 24-hour vertical videos/pictures are a fast, authentic way to show behind the scenes. I met Jon Youshaei, IGTV's marketing manager, at Vidcon. He said that Instagram is focusing on promoting videos through stories and IGTV. A year or two ago, users mainly checked the feed. Youshaei predicts users will check stories more, and stories will thus have a more prominent role in the Instagram experience. This is enormously valuable to know as a company: Make sure to post in stories to stay on top of your Instagram game.

Instagram optimization tips

Always my first advice: Make relevant video content your viewers want to watch *specifically on Instagram.* Next, a few more tips to optimize your Instagram videos.

Interaction

Work on relationships and interaction. Make sure to stay on top of likes, comments, and direct messages between you and your ideal viewers.

Hashtags, locations

Use relevant hashtags and locations so people can find your content. According to SproutSocial, nine hashtags are ideal on Instagram posts.

Tag people and companies

Tag relevant people and businesses in your posts and stories. If you tag people or companies, there is a good chance those people or that company will like or comment on your video – they might even share it. But be careful with tagging too many people or companies; you don't want to be seen as a spammer.

"Videos in your Instagram Stories let your followers experience what's happening here and now. Make them as real as possible, not too perfect, and take people along in your story. Use fun interactive elements, such as the poll, question, and emoji slider to get more interaction."
Kirsten Jassies, Instagram Expert

Make stories

Make stories on a regular basis. Instagram stories are a fast, easy way to put your brand back on top of your target audience's updates. Remember to use the locations, hashtags, and interactive tools in your stories for interaction and to get the stories found.

Livestream

Ready for the next step? Do a livestream! My two big rules for livestreaming are to have a good reason to go live, and to prepare well. Livestreaming works very well on Instagram because as soon as you go live, your followers will get a notification, and your account is on top of their stories feeds.

Right timing

Post your videos when your target audience is online. According to SproutSocial, Wednesday is the ideal day to post on Instagram (specifically at 11 o'clock in the morning). But like I mentioned before, this differs per target audience, so experiment with the right day and time for your audience.

Instagram audit

Do you want to get more insight into your Instagram account? A quick check at igaudit.io can tell you the basics of how you're doing: average number of likes, interaction, number of fake followers, and language of your followers.

For a bit more in depth: For what you're doing well as a brand and where there are areas for improvement, check Iconosquare's free Instagram Audit for business accounts. It looks at the last 30 days of your posts, and your overall profile. After that, of course, you will be asked to subscribe to Iconosquare, where you can gain insight into all sorts of interesting statistics: interaction, followers, stories data, etc.

FACEBOOK PUBLICATION GUIDELINES

Facebook has undergone many changes and developments in recent years. I remember creating a Facebook account as a student in the United States in 2005. At that time, Facebook was a new, trendy network to keep in touch with fellow students.

Nowadays, Facebook is definitely not new anymore; everyone and their grandmother has a Facebook account. Facebook remains a huge platform, where millions of people stay in touch, close communities exist, games are played, and business video can lead to many impressions and much interaction.

When to post on Facebook

The biggest question before posting on Facebook: Is your target audience active on Facebook? And I need to emphasize the word active here, because there are a lot of people with a Facebook account who do not actively use it.

If your ideal viewers are active on Facebook, how are you then able to use video to reach that audience? What type of content is your target audience waiting for?

The two video categories that get the most interaction on Facebook are current events and entertainment. So, make a video that entertains people, or make something that benefits them at that particular time. Almost half of all Americans get their news from Facebook. Do you know what is currently relevant for your target audience? What does your ideal viewer have questions about? Are there themes that are currently trending? Did something recently happen, or is something going to happen that your viewer would like to be informed about?

"Since I'm doing video in my professional Facebook group, the positive feedback is awesome! From now on it's just me, my brand new tripod and my camera."
Kim Swagemakers, Social Media & List Building Expert

Facebook algorithm

As with each network, the first step in being visible on Facebook is by having good content. This is the foundation of optimizing every video and retaining your viewer's attention. There is no point in optimizing keywords, tags, and description if the video itself is not worth watching. Facebook's algorithm mainly looks at:

Viewer loyalty & intent

Facebook says that it gives more weight in its ranking to pages and videos that people keep coming back to. You could, for example, create a video series that continues every other day or every week.

Video and view length

Facebook has a strong preference for videos that appeal –
videos that hold the viewer's attention and ensure more
interaction. So, videos that are viewed for a long time have
priority over videos that have a short viewing time.
Facebook even indicates that the video duration should
ideally be longer than three minutes. My advice is to match
the duration of the video to your message and the ideal
viewer.

Originality

Facebook says that originality is rewarded. The platform
appreciates creators who produce original content. So,
make your own original content instead of just sharing and
reposting other people's videos.

The ranking of your Facebook video mainly depends on:
- The number of shares (authentic shares).
- The amount of interaction on the video.
- Whether the video sparks conversation.

Optimizing your video for Facebook comes down to having
a good video that people watch for a long time, and also do
something with: share, comment, like. That's the
foundation!

Practical Facebook optimization tips

Unique content that sparks conversation

Create unique videos that people watch for a long time. Don't share other people's videos but make your own distinctive videos that spark interaction between Facebook users. This can be interaction in the public feed, but it can also be private conversations between users. Make videos that teach viewers something, that entertain them, or that are inspiring. These are the kinds of videos that make people tag friends and start a conversation.

Returning viewers

Make videos that ensure viewers come back to your page. This can work well with a video series. It can also be helpful to have a fixed day and time of publication.

Save the best for the beginning

On Facebook, most people won't find your video by searching for it. They will probably stumble upon it in their feed. Because viewers are scrolling in their feeds and not intentionally looking for your video, you need to grab their attention at the start of the video. So put your best shot, best statement, or most moving quote at the start of the video.

Design your video for sound off

Most of the videos on Facebook are watched without audio (85%). So, before publishing, watch your video without audio. Does your message still come across? Use captions and/or graphics to make sure your viewers keep watching.

Livestream

Use livestreams to get the attention of your ideal target audience. Viewers on average stay three times longer with a live video than a regular video on Facebook. My two rules of thumb for live-streaming: Have a good reason to go live, and prepare very well.

"The best way to engage your audience and expand your influence on Facebook is to use live video! With Facebook live, you can deepen your relationship with your audience instantly by connecting to them on a more human level! And you don't need fancy equipment to get started - you can do it from your phone!"
Luria Petrucci, Livestream expert

Optimize for mobile

Keep in mind that 80% of Facebook users are on their phone. Chances are your video is being watched from a small screen. Make sure the text and captions are large enough for small screens, use closeup shots, and check your video on your own device before publishing it.

VIDEO STATISTICS & ADJUSTING STRATEGY

At the start of a video training I always ask: "Who regularly makes videos?" Usually, most hands will go up. Then I ask the question: "Who regularly checks their video statistics?" And as fast as all hands went up, they all go down.

Are you on track?

How interesting is that? If you have a goal (see chapter one), doesn't it make sense to check whether you're on track to reach that goal? Say you want to lose weight. You make a plan and start running every other day. You then probably also want to know whether your runs are working, by weighing yourself every once in a while.

The same goes for your video strategy. You probably created a video vision and video plan after the first chapter of this book. After production is done, be sure to schedule a moment (once every 14 days, for example) to dive into your video statistics.

Who watches your videos?

And by that I don't just mean the views, but deeper: Who watches your video? Is it your target audience, your ideal viewers you had in mind in your video vision and video plan? How long do people keep watching your videos? Does that match the initial plan? Do they use a laptop, or do they watch from a mobile device? All of these statistics tell you a lot about your viewers, their behaviors, and if your initial plan is actually working.

Of course, different networks will give you different insights in views and the behavior of your viewers. Still, with a few basic statistics, you're able to get to know your viewers and determine if your video strategy is working. If you have placed a certain video on multiple social channels, you can also see where it did best and where it did worse. But keep in mind that each network measures its statistics differently.

Understand your statistics

An organic view on Facebook, for example, is counted at three seconds; on Instagram Stories, it's as soon as it is opened; and on YouTube, it's usually around 30 seconds. (Measuring views on YouTube is a complicated, different story. Check my YouTube channel if you want to know how it works.)

My advice is to set a fixed moment to check out and analyze the video statistics. Only then will you know whether the current video approach works, or whether you need to make adjustments. Because isn't that what you initially set up to do? You had a goal in mind. You created a video with that goal in mind. Make sure to stick with that plan!

EPILOGUE

The best way to learn to make good business videos? By making lots of videos. Just start somewhere. That's how you learn!

And it doesn't have to be complicated. In fact, it has never been this easy to make a video. Grab your phone, hit record, and upload. But because it is so accessible, there are many videos made and uploaded that no one watches: videos that don't have a clear goal, videos where the audio or light is distracting, or videos that simply just never reach their target audience.

In this book I have laid the foundation for making business videos with your phone in five steps. You always start with a basic video plan (chapter 1). After that, shoot your video using the filming tips from chapter 2. While standing in front of the camera, always keep your ideal viewer in mind (chapter 3). Then you edit the video simply with an app on your phone (chapter 4). Because you had a clear video plan, you can now also place and optimize your video on the right platform (chapter 5).

Practice with techniques in front of the camera, techniques behind the camera, practice with cool video editing apps, but most of all: keep practicing. Get that camera out of your pocket, and start making videos. Weekend getaway? Make a video. Your child's first step? Make a video. Nice networking event? Video!

Just keep DOING it. The more you do it, the more my tips will become a routine. And the more fun you will have!

On my website, you can find all kinds of training tools to master the above steps. From your own video coach to an extensive online academy with all kinds of video tutorials – all the tools and knowledge you need to make effective business videos yourself are there.

I warmly invite you to become part of this growing community of *videogeeks*.

But most of all, I wish you the best of luck (and fun!) with making your own business videos.

Happy filming!

Pelpina

SOURCES

A big thank you to the bright minds I was able to interview and quote in this book. Here are some further sources to read/watch more on video statistics, formats and social media marketing:

Bond, C. (June 7, 2020) *Boost your Facebook Video Views with These 6 Tactics.* https://www.wordstream.com/blog/ws/2020/01/30/faceboo k-video-views

Carey-Simos, G. (February 21, 2019) *Which is better: vertical or square video?* Wersm.com https://wersm.com/which-is-better-vertical-video-or-square-video/

Dupuis, T. (June 20, 2020) *YouTube SEO: How To Optimize Your Videos To Rank Higher In Both YouTube And Google* https://onlinemediamasters.com/youtube-video-seo/

Iqbal, M. (June 23, 2020) *Instagram Revenue and Usage Statistics (2020).* Businessofapps.com https://www.businessofapps.com/data/instagram-statistics/

Osman, M. (April 10, 2020) *Mindblowing LinkedIn Statistics and Facts*. Kinsta.com https://kinsta.com/blog/linkedin-statistics/

Mialki, S. (January 25, 2019) *LinkedIn Video Ads: Best Practices, Examples and Ad Specs (Free Guide)* Instapage.com https://instapage.com/blog/linkedin-video-ads#:~:text=Create%20video%20content%20based%20on%20your%20objective&text=For%20brand%20awareness%20%E2%80%94%20Share%20about,lift%20in%20view%20completion%20rates.

Peters, B. (February 19, 2019). *Does vertical video make a difference? We spent $6000 to find out.* Buffer.com https://buffer.com/resources/vertical-video/

Zalani, C. (May 31, 2020) *The state of video marketing in 2020.* Socialmediatoday.com https://www.socialmediatoday.com/news/the-state-of-video-marketing-in-2020-infographic/578888/

Zarzycki, K. & Cyca, M. (April 13, 2020) *The complete guide to social media video specs in 2020.* Blog.hootsuite.com https://blog.hootsuite.com/social-media-video-specs/

ABOUT THE AUTHOR

Pelpina helps companies generate visibility, sales and authority by creating videos with impact. She has trained thousands of professionals worldwide to create videos using smartphones.

Pelpina offers a unique combination of expertise with years of experience in journalism, TV, and online video, combined with practical knowledge on apps, social media, and content marketing.

On any regular day, you can find Pelpina hosting a video, filming, editing, making video strategy plans, and sharing her knowledge through training, speaking, and (online) coaching. Find more on Pelpina at Pelpina.com

9 789083 088006